The Mirror of Production

The Mirror of Production

by Jean Baudrillard

Translated with "Introduction"

by Mark Poster

TELOS PRESS • ST. LOUIS

Published originally as *Le Miroir de la Production*.
English translation copyright © 1975 by *Telos Press*.
All rights reserved.

ISBN: 0-914386-06-9

Library of Congress: 74-82994

Manufactured in the United States of America.

TABLE OF CONTENTS

TRANSLATOR'S INTRODUCTION

For some time now many of us have harbored the knowledge or at least the suspicion that Marxism is an inadequate perspective for the critical analysis of advanced society. We have toyed with syntheses, those of the Frankfurt School, of the Italian phenomenological Marxists, of the Freudo-Marxists, of the French existential Marxists without completely satisfying results. Radicals who prefer action to theory also bear witness to the impasse of Marxism by their frantic flight from advanced society under the changing banner of some Hero of the colonized peoples, Ho Chi Minh, Che Guevarra, Mao and now Stalin himself. In this conjuncture Jean Baudrillard, in *The Mirrow of Production*, has attempted a radical deconstruction of Marxism along with an alternative standpoint for today's radicalism.

In *The Mirror of Production* (1973), Baudrillard marshalls his earlier analyses from *Le systèm des objets* (1968), *La société de consommation* (1970) and *Pour une critique de l'économie politique du signe* (1972) for a systematic critique of Marxism. His compelling conclusion is that Marx's theory of historical materialism, whether it is attributed to the *1844 Manuscripts*, to the *German Ideology*, to *Capital*, or to the entire corpus, is too conservative, too rooted in the assumptions of political economy, too dependent on the system of ideas that it seeks to overthrow to provide a framework for radical action. The fatal weakness in Marx comes not from his effort to outline a revolutionary social theory — Baudrillard does not dispute this imperative — but in the failure of historical materialism to attain this end.

For Baudrillard the conceptual grounds upon which Marx laid his critique of political economy were the "forms" of production and labor, forms that Marx did not subject to criticism and which were, in origin, those of political economy itself. When Marx unmasked an anthropology of needs and of use value behind the system of exchange value he was not transcending political economy but merely seeing its reverse side. Selecting representative quotes from the entire scope of Marx's texts, from the *Critique of Hegel's Philosophy of Right* to the *Notes on Wagner*, Baudrillard argues that Marx's effort to plumb the "apparent movement of political economy" in order to reverse its theoretical flow in which use value derived from exchange value, far from dismantling political economy, only completed and "interiorized" it. Hence Marx's argument against "abstract labor" by reference to "concrete" labor still relied on the rationalist Western concept of labor itself. In both cases "social wealth" is still conceived in terms of a universal activity of man, i.e., labor, that imposes an arbitrary, rationalist intentionality on all human activity. Benjamin Franklin and Marx agree that "man" is a "tool-making" animal.

New Left theorists have not often systematically interrogated Marx himself. The theory of historical materialism has not often been analyzed to see if its emphases and directions might not systematically

obscure the contemporary social field. It is precisely
this task that Baudrillard sets for himself and his
judgment is severe: "...Marxism assists the ruse of
capital. It convinces men that they are alienated by
the sale of their labor power; hence it censors the
much more radical hypothesis that they do not have
to be the labor power, the 'unalienable' power of
creating value by their labor." Far from transcending political economy, Marxism, to Baudrillard, strengthens and extends its most basic propositions. Man is conceptualized as a producing animal
just as in political economy, except that Marx wants
to liberate his productive potential. This still leaves
us with a metaphor or "mirror" of production
through which alone every aspect of social activity is
intelligible. And so contemporary French theorists
remain trapped in this conceptual cage: Althusser
sees theory as a "production," Deleuze and Guattari
give us an unconscious that is a "producer" of desire,
the *Tel Quel* group refers to textual "production."

But it was political economy that erected that
"phantasm," in Baudrillard's words, of labor as the
human essence. To whatever extent Marx was able
to demystify its liberal usage, to extract it from the
hegemony of bourgeois rule, he still turned it over
to the working class, imposed it on them, as their
central means of self-comprehension. Baudrillard
would like to liberate the workers from their "labor
power," to have them, if they are to represent a
radical alternative to the present system, think
themselves under another sign than that of
production.

Marx's concept of labor is, in its deepest levels,
identified with that of political economy. Man is
confronted by nature as a natural necessity which he

must act upon. Man does this by investing nature with value, a value that he then extracts. The scheme is one in which labor power utilizes technology to compel nature to yield its riches for human enjoyment. Both political economy and Marxism are at one here. Baudrillard points out that there is no symbolic exchange in this perspective, there is no reciprocal play of meanings and acts. Labor and nature are both reduced to "values" that require the proper means (technology) to actualize. Political economy might idealize labor into an individualist morality whereas historical materialism might materialize it in a notion of fulfillment: But both participate in the same anthropology of man seeking his telos in the conquest of nature, an anthropology that becomes mystifying when the system begins to create ecological catastrophes. Baudrillard argues that "By positing use value as the beyond of exchange value, one locks all transcendence into the single, internal alternative of the field of value. But qualitative production is now the realm of rational, positive finality; the transformation of nature is now the place of its objectification as a productive force under the sign of utility (the same is simultaneously true of human labor). Even before the stage of exchange value and of the equivalent time of abstract social labor, labor and production already constitute an abstraction, a reduction and an outrageous rationalization in the relation to the richness of symbolic exchange." A utilitarian hypothesis encompasses the human project and nature, one that is arbitrary and unjustified, in both political economy and its critique.

What is at stake in Baudrillard's critique of Marx is the gravitational center of the system of political

economy. For Marx, the primary place (determinant
instance) of capitalism is in the structure of the
means of production and the relations of
production. Over against political economy, which
sought the deep structure of capitalism in the process
of exchange value, in the determination of the price
of the commodity through the "free" intercourse of
demands and supplies, Marx shifted the center
toward the "real" act of the production and the
consumption of products. But for Baudrillard, in
both cases the real logic is the same: it is the investment of things with value; it is the placing of a sign ✕
on a thing and the logic of this process of
signification is the true essence of capital. The
difference between Marx and political economy is
not as great as their agreement. The Marxist critique
unmasked the "abstractions" of exchange value in
favor of the "concrete" processes of use value, of
production and labor. But Marx's concepts were not
at all radical; they did not reach the root of the
matter. All Marx did was to set forth the repressed
side of the equations of political economy. Instead of
the shadows of the market place, we are sent to an
equally obscure underside of the system: the place
of production. Following this displacement of the
center of the system to its "human side," Marx
unravelled the threads of the entire social field
through the "mirror of production," at the same
time unmasking the exploitative nature of the
system. Instead of the "justice" of exchange equivalence, we have the unjust extraction of
surplus-value fom the laborer, or, alternatively, the
alienation of his life energies. In the process of
Marx's analysis, however, the social sphere is

filtered, inexorably, through the concepts of
production and labor which become the unquestioned metaphysical reference points of social
reality.

The problem is not that Marx is an economic
determinist, that he does not value highly enough
the "finer" aspects of human culture. It is not a
question of replacing a "materialist" theory with an
"idealist" one. Rather, the problem is that he did not
penetrate the central logic of political economy,
which is, to Baudrillard, its logic of signification.
Marx theorized the origin of political economy as a
transformation of the mode of production and
relations of production. But there has been a second
decisive change in political economy that Marx did
not recognize and this involved a "process of social
abstraction" that refers not to the commodity but to
the sign. The chief merit of Baudrillard's thought is
to articulate a critique of the political economy of
the sign which he regards as the dominant social
form of advanced capitalism. Political economy had
generated its mode of signification from the outset,
during the Renaissance, but Marx was unable to
theorize this object because first, like Ricardo and
the others, he was tied to the mirror of production,
and, second, because his discourse, like theirs, was
representational and hence incapable of seeing the
radically new form of social exchanges.

Baudrillard employs the concepts of contemporary structural linguistics to develop his critique.
Structuralists break down the linguistic sign into a
signifier (a language term), a signified (an intended
meaning), and a referent (an object pointed to by
the signifier). Structuralists merely theorize the
signifier, in search of its systematic quality,

relegating the signified and the referent to an obscure horizon of their science. What they have been able to do is to show that signifiers have become abstracted from the subject (the signified) and from the social world of objects (the referent). While they claim this situation is natural and inevitable, Baudrillard argues that the essence of political economy is precisely this separation; the increasing autonomization of the signifier not simply in the realm of language but in all aspects of social exchange. Marx foresaw that capitalism would corrupt all values, moral, cultural, sexual, etc., by the force of the exchange value of the commodity. Baudrillard asserts that the strategy of the capitalist system is to generate this abstract structure of signification of which the commodity is merely one example. What happens in political economy is this: "the signified and the referent are now abolished to the sole profit of the play of signifiers, of a generalized formalization where the code no longer refers back to any subjective or objective 'reality,' but to its own logic. The signifier becomes its own referent and the use value of the sign disappears to the profit only of its commutation and exchange value. The sign no longer designates anything at all. It approaches in its truth its structural limit which is to refer back only to other signs. All reality then becomes the place of a semiological manipulation, of a structural simulation. And whereas the traditional sign...is the object of a conscious investment, of a rational calculation of signifieds, here it is the code that becomes the instance of absolute reference." Here we are beyond the stable bourgeois world of the nineteenth century where the consumer carefully weighed his money against the value of the commodity, carefully estimated his need against his resources. This stable, comfortable, knowable world where words clearly referred to things, where ideas represented reality, where values corresponded to needs, where commodities had unquestioned value, was the world of Marx and his thought. There could simply not be articulated a "revolution" in underarm deodorants, the incorporation (imaginary or real) of personal qualities through the purchase of commodities, or a "clean bomb." Baudrillard's critique of the sign allows him to render the situation of advanced capitalism with much more concreteness than traditional Marxism. Whole realms of contemporary protest (Blacks, Women, Youth, etc.) and critique (consumption, sex, language, the media, etc.) can be seen better in relation to the repressiveness of the code than in relation to the mode of production. The dramatic tension in the system comes from its difficulty in reproducing the code, while production itself becomes merely an ideological support of the system. (It delivers the goods.)

In *Le systém des objets*, Baudrillard analyzed consumption through a critique of the sign. The prejudice in favor of production as the active moment and consumption as passive originated with the political economy but was confirmed by Marx. This productivist ideology produces an absence in social theory: it cannot account for the articulated complexity of a symbolic exchange in consumption. Baudrillard asserts that consumption is as "active" an exchange as production. In consumption there is an active appropriation of signs, not the simple destruction of an object. What is consumed is not simply a material object that satisfies an all too rational need, but a symbolic meaning in which the consumer places himself in a communication structure where an exchange occurs which is profoundly tied to the whole system of political economy. In order for the system to be reproduced there must be not simply the reproduction of labor power but the continuous reproduction of the code.

To Baudrillard, the present system of signs in consumption entails a serious distortion of human exchange. Under political economy, every level of social exchange is reduced from symbolic reciprocity to the "terrorism" of the "code." Baudrillard's critique of political economy leads not simply to another productivist ideology, but penetrates the system in a radical way: the abstraction from the symbolic reciprocity of exchanges to the abstract, discontinuous manipulation of the code. It is the very genius of political economy, a genius that makes it immune to traditional Marxist critiques, that the signs exchanged in communication have no referent. Capitalism detaches the signifier from the signified, making the signifier its own signified. What is crucial about, say, a given underarm deodorant, is not that it has a given exchange value or a given use value, not that the workers who produced it were alienated or exploited. The secret of this commodity is that it can totally transcend all of these "referents," that it can become a totally detached object of exchange and that the person who consumes it can find a "meaning" in it to be appropriated that is totally divorced from the mechanisms of production and distribution. What is consumed is not a thing, laden with materiality and the complex cycle that finally derives from labor and nature, but purely and simply an element in a code. ⚹

There can be no internal contradiction endangering the system of monopoly capital because, as long as it controls the code, consumption can be indefinitely extended. There is no referent against which to define a finitude of needs because the code is its own referent and there is no end to the consumption of the code. As long as the code is not dismantled, there will be no difficulty for the system in getting workers to produce. Hence production is no longer the locus of the contradiction. In Baudrillard's analysis, the very form of social meanings becomes the central articulation of social theory, not as a pure form but as a structured form that is in movement, in transition. His theory avoids the mistake of having the theoretical model divided into aspects (economic, politics, ideology) that are those of the dominant ideology itself. He is adept at exposing the pitfalls of historical materialism when it seeks to comprehend pre-capitalist structures: for example, Godelier's stumbling acrobatics in his concepts of structure in dominance and determinant instance.

Yet, there are serious difficulties with Baudrillard's position. Over against the sign structure of political economy, its code, he counterposes something that he calls "symbolic exchange." Henri Lefebvre has argued that capitalism's structure employs "signals" increasingly in order to command integration and acceptance. By collapsing the signified into the signifier, the signal leaves no room for judgment or criticism, as in the statement "We are in the Free World." He opposed the spoken word (*la parole*) to signals denoting a free structure of face-to-face discourse. Baudrillard moves in the same direction as Lefebvre, with many of the same difficulties. Advanced capitalism creates places of "non-marked" terms (Blacks, women, youth, those on welfare). These groups are defined by their lack of responsibility, and hence, they are at a "zero point" of the code where their speech does not count. Thus, they are in a truly radical position because they must oppose not simply an inequality in the code, but the code itself. And they do so, as in the French events of May, 1968, by a spontaneous resort to *la parole*.

In the act of speech there is a reciprocal giving and taking of meanings that transcend the abstraction and manipulation of the sign. There is a discharge of energy and meaning, a pure loss as well as a gain. This is the essence of symbolic exchange to Baudrillard. In political economy, on the contrary, there is never a loss; everything, even war, always results in an accumulation of value, a re-investment. This is the secret of capitalism as compared with other systems: its inexorable growth. Even when it tries to give some of its value away, to share power through participation becomes co-optation. Symbolic exchange is simply impossible as the system was designed precisely to destroy it through a long process of abstraction and separation. Yet, this celebration of *la parole* implies a false assumption about the total presence of the exchangers. It implies an ontology of centered presence; as Baudrillard says, "we are always totally there." Perhaps there is some dialectic of presence and absence that could account for miscomprehension as well as for symbolic exchange in social interactions. But Baudrillard had not given it to us.

There are strong echoes of the Frankfurt School in

Baudrillard. He designates the same groups as
Marcuse as the radical edge of the system; he
employs Marcuse's concepts like repressive desublimation; and he speaks like Marcuse of a "refusal" as
the revolutionary act. But there are still more
theoretical affinities with Habermas. The resort to
symbolic exchange is like the German's effort to
complement the concept of labor with the concept of
symbolic interaction, to addend Weber to Marx.
Yet, with the background of French structuralism,
Baudrillard is able to re-conceptualize the structure
of society in a way in which Habermas is not. For the
latter, symbolic interaction is added to labor, whereas for Baudrillard the whole theoretical object shifts
in its nature. In a later phase of his thought,
Habermas employs a notion of an ideal-speaking situation, enlisting a concept of communication in the
critical theory of society. This, of course, is very close
to the concept of *la parole* in Baudrillard and both
suffer from serious weaknesses in political implication. In sum, there are deep confluences in two of
the main centers of contemporary critical theory.

For Baudrillard, as for the Frankfurt School,
there is a major problem of defining the limits of
Marx's achievement. In France, Baudrillard's
reading of Marx's texts is unusual in that it does not
divide them up, favoring one group or another.
Instead, he criticizes Marx on the basis of a claim
against themes that exist throughout the corpus.
While in the 1950s in France there was a fascination
with the early texts, especially the *1844 Manuscripts*,
by humanists, Catholics, existentialists and independent Marxists, the more recent trend, that of
Althusser's circle, has been to reject the early Marx
in favor of a "mature" Marx who is placed at a later

and later date in his career. By stressing the unity of the texts, even if it is a unity to be criticized, Baudrillard returns us to an integral view of Marx.

Baudrillard's attitude toward Marx is deeply ambivalent. In *Pour une critique de l'économie politique du signe* he placed himself squarely within Marxist thought as one who was pursuing further the critique of political economy. But in *The Mirror of Production* there are places where Marx is completely rejected. This comes through in the sections he devotes to epistemology, sections that conclude each chapter. His effort is to call into question the nature of the theoretical model of historical materialism, not simply its contents. The charge against Marx is not so much that he imposed his concept of production on precapitalist societies where it has no place, but that historical materialism becomes ideological when it forgets its historical limits and pretends to universality, an error that is characteristic of the whole tradition of Western thought. The problem is not simply one of a lapse of memory, a momentary theoretical slippage, but, Baudrillard argues, one that is implicit in the deepest epistemological premises of Marx. The first error derives from Marx's Hegelianism which asserts an overly absolute truth value to historical materialism because capitalism creates the conditions for universal, scientific knowledge. Ironically, this is the Althusserian position that attributes to Marxist knowledge the quality of finality. All of history can be objectively read by Marxism because of a favored historical position. With this claim Marxism gives up its own self-relativization: it is dependent upon a certain historical conjuncture, but at the same time, this conjuncture affords it an absolute priority over all previous ages. Marxism becomes ideological not where Althusser thinks, in its relation to practice, but in its truth claims, its scientificity. This problem has been raised many times before and needs no commentary here.

But there is a second difficulty that Baudrillard outlines. Marx erects a "model" of social structure and social change and Baudrillard objects to the analytic nature of Marxist concepts. Not only does capitalism fail to provide a standpoint for a universal theory, but it does not even offer the critical theorist the perspective from which to comprehend earlier societies. It is illegitimate for Marxism to project its notion of the mode of production onto earlier social systems. In this charge Baudrillard has placed himself on theoretical thin ice.

He wants to say that the Marxist model misses the radicality of the difference between earlier societies and capitalism as well as the radicality that would make a difference between capitalism and a future society all because of its analytic model. The model of production prevents a sighting of the symbolic nature of exchanges in primitive society; it absorbs that society into its own likeness and projects a vision of it back only in its relative difference, its underdeveloped mode of production. But to claim that this inadequacy in Marxism is due to the analytic nature of its concepts and to claim that a standpoint in the present, however critical, provides no basis for illuminating past structures courts the danger of pure relativism. The difficulty that Baudrillard presents is that of how to make radical discontinuities intelligible. He wants to claim a deep rupture between primitive society and political economy; but historical, analytic models make intelligible only continuities or relative differences.

For his own part, Baudrillard presents a history of social systems that in barest outline goes from pre-industrial societies of symbolic exchange, to political economy, and then to a third phase in which the full development of political economy is reached in the complete negation of symbolism. A fourth stage is implied in which we return to symbolism. This history is marked by discontinuity and itself implies an analytic of signification systems; but neither of these elements are theorized by Baudrillard. In other words, the incompleteness and obscurities of his critique of the epistemology of historical materialism return and emerge in his own standpoint. The direction of his critique is well taken: the inherent teleology in Marxism and its overly continuous model are open to attack. But Baudrillard has not shown us the way toward a discontinuous model that avoids finalizing all history in the present but allows for some sort of totalization, however fragmentary, that provides for a critical standpoint that can illuminate current practice. His failure here leaves him with only an empty invocation for a spontaneous overthrow of the code à la May, 1968.

All in all, Baudrillard's hypothesis of a critique of the political economy of the sign offers a promising direction for radical theory. It combines semiology with a notion of everyday life that increasingly appear to offer the best options for theoretical development.

Mark Poster
Irvine, California

PREFACE

A specter haunts the revolutionary imagination:
the phantom of production. Everywhere it sustains
an unbridled romanticism of productivity. The
critical theory of the *mode* of production does not
touch the *principle* of production. All the concepts it
articulates describe only the dialectical and
historical genealogy of the *contents* of production,
leaving production as a *form* intact. This form
reemerges, idealized, behind the critique of the
capitalist mode of production. Through a strange
contagion, this form of production only reinforces
revolutionary discourse as a language of productivity. From the liberation of productive forces in the
unlimited "textual productivity" of *Tel Quel* to
Deleuze's factory-machine productivity of the
unconscious (including the "labor" of the unconscious), no revolution can place itself under any
other sign. The general formula is that of a
productive Eros. Social wealth or language, meaning
or value, sign or phantasm—everything is "produced" according to a "labor." If this is the truth of
capital and of political economy, it is taken up whole
by the revolution only to capital's benefit. The
capitalist system of production is to be subverted in
the name of an authentic and radical productivity.
The capitalist law of value is to be abolished in
the name of a de-alienated hyperproductivity,
a productive hyperspace. Capital develops the

productive forces but also restrains them: they must be liberated. The exchange of signifieds has always hidden the "labor" of the signifier: let us liberate the signifier and the textual production of meaning! The unconscious is surrounded in social, linguistic, and Oedipal structures: let us give it back its brute energy; let us restore it as a productive machine! Everywhere productivist discourse reigns and, whether this productivity has objective ends or is deployed for itself, it is itself the form of value. It is the leitmotif both of the system and of a radical challenge — but such a consensus is suspect. If the discourse of production is only a revolutionary metaphor — the detour and return of a concept which, in essence, emanates from political economy and obeys its reality principle — then this metaphor is dangerous if it is to designate a radical alternative. Or if the alternative is not radical and its contamination by productivist discourse signifies more than a metaphoric infection, the virtual impossibility of thinking beyond or outside the general scheme of production, then it is in counter-dependence on the dominant scheme.[1]

But isn't this dominant scheme, which metaphorizes all azimuths, itself merely a metaphor? Is the reality principle it imposes anything but a code, a cipher, or a system of interpretation? Marx shattered the fiction of *homo economicus*, the myth which sums up the whole process of the naturalization of

---

1. Evidently Marx played an essential role in the rooting of this productivist metaphor. It was he who definitively radicalized and rationalized the concept of production, who "dialectized" it and gave it its revolutionary title of nobility. And it is in large part by unconditional reference to Marx that this concept pursues its prodigious career.

the system of exchange value, the market, and
surplus value and its forms. But he did so in the
name of labor power's emergence in action, of man's
own power to give rise to value by his labor
(*pro-ducere*). Isn't this a similar fiction, a similar
naturalization — another wholly arbitrary conven-
tion, a simulation model bound to *code* all human
material and every contingency of desire and
exchange in terms of value, finality, and
production? If so, production would be nothing but
a code imposing this type of decipherment, *the*
decipherment, where there is properly neither
finality, cipher, nor value. In rational terms, this
gigantic secondary elaboration hallucinates man's
predestination for the objective transformation of
the world (or for the "production" of oneself: today's
generalized humanist theme — it is no longer a
question of "being" oneself but of "producing"
oneself, from conscious activity to the primitive
"productions" of desire. Everywhere man has
learned to reflect on himself, to assume himself, to
posit himself according to this scheme of production
which is assigned to him as the ultimate dimension of
value and meaning. At the level of all political
economy there is something of what Lacan describes
in the mirror stage: through this scheme of
production, this *mirror* of production, the human
species comes to consciousness [*la prise de
conscience*] *in the imaginary*. Production, labor,
value, everything through which an objective world
emerges and through which man recognizes himself
objectively — this is the imaginary. Here man is
embarked on a continual deciphering of himself
through his works, finalized by his shadow (his own
end), reflected by this operational mirror, this sort of
ideal of a productivist ego. This process occurs not

only in the materialized form of an economic obsession with efficiency determined by the *system* of exchange value, but more profoundly in this *overdetermination by the code*, by the mirror of political economy: in the identity that man dons with his own eyes when he can think of himself only as something to produce, to transform, or bring about as value. This remarkable phantasm is confused with that of representation, in which man becomes his own *signified* for himself and enjoys himself as the *content* of value and meaning in a process of self-expression and self-accumulation whose form escapes him.

It is further clarified (despite the exegetical prowess of structuralist Marxists) that the analysis of the form representation (the status of the sign, of the language that directs all Western thought)—the critical reduction of this form in its collusion with the order of production and political economy—escaped Marx. It is no longer worthwhile to make a radical critique of the order of representation in the name of production and of its revolutionary formula. These two orders are inseparable and, paradoxical though it may seem, Marx did not subject *the form production to a radical analysis any more than he did the form representation*. These are the two great unanalyzed forms of the imaginary[2] of political economy that imposed their limits on him. The discourse of production and the discourse of representation are the mirror by which the system of political economy comes to be reflected in the imaginary and reproduced there as the determinant instance.

---

2. A term developed by Jacques Lacan and later used by C. Castoriadis to denote collective values that provide for unitary meaning but are logically unprovable. [Translator's note]

I. THE CONCEPT OF LABOR

In order to achieve a radical critique of political economy, it is not enough to unmask what is hidden behind the concept of consumption: the anthropology of needs and of use value. We must also unmask everything hidden behind the concepts of production, mode of production, productive forces, relations of production, etc. All the fundamental concepts of Marxist analysis must be questioned, starting from its own requirement of a radical critique and transcendence of political economy. What is axiomatic about productive forces or about the dialectical genesis of modes of production from which springs all revolutionary theory? What is axiomatic about the generic richness of man who is labor power, about the motor of history, or about history itself, which is only "the production by men of their material life?" "The first historical act is thus the production of the means to satisfy these needs, the production of material life itself. And indeed this is an historical act, a fundamental condition of all history, which today, as thousands of years ago, must daily and hourly be fulfilled merely in order to sustain human life."[1]

The liberation of productive forces is confused with the liberation of man: is this a revolutionary

---

1. *The German Ideology* (New York: International Publishers, 1947), p. 16.

formula or that of political economy itself? Almost
no one has doubted such ultimate evidence,
especially not Marx, for whom men "begin to
distinguish themselves from animals as soon as they
begin to *produce* their means of subsistence..."[2]
(Why must man's vocation always be to distinguish
himself from animals? Humanism is an *idée fixe*
which also comes from political economy—but we
will leave that for now.) But is man's existence an
end for which he must find the means? These
innocent little phrases are already theoretical
conclusions: the separation of the end from the
means is the wildest and most naive postulate about
the human race. Man has needs. Does he have
needs? Is he pledged to satisfy them? Is he labor
power (by which he separates himself as means from
himself as his own end)? These prodigious metaphors
of the system that dominates us are a fable of
political economy retold to generations of revolutionaries infected even in their political radicalism
by the conceptual viruses of this same political
economy.

Critique of Use Value and Labor Power

In the distinction between exchange value and use
value, Marxism shows its strength but also its
weakness. The presupposition of use value—the
hypothesis of a concrete value beyond the
abstraction of exchange value, a human purpose of
the commodity in the moment of its direct relation
of utility for a subject—is only the effect of the system of exchange value, a concept produced and

----

2.   *Ibid.,* p. 7.

developed by it.[3] Far from designating a realm beyond political economy, use value is only the horizon of exchange value. A radical questioning of the concept of consumption begins at the level of needs and products. *But this critique attains its full scope in its extension to that other commodity, labor power.* It is the concept of production, then, which is submitted to a radical critique.

We must not forget that according to Marx himself the revolutionary originality of his theory comes from releasing the concept of labor power from its status as an unusual commodity whose insertion in the cycle of production *under the name of use value* carries the X element, a differential extra-value that generates surplus value and the whole process of capital. (Bourgeois economics would think instead of simple "labor" as one factor of production among others in the economic process.)

The history of Marx's concept of the use value of labor power is complex. With the concept of labor, Adam Smith attacked the Physiocrats and the exchangists. In turn, Marx deconstructed labor into a double concept of labor power commodity: abstract social labor (exchange value) and concrete labor (use value). He insisted on the need to maintain these two aspects in all their force. Their articulation alone could help decipher objectively the process of capitalist labor. To A. Wagner, who reproached him for neglecting use value, Marx replied: "...the *vir obscurus* overlooks the fact that even in the analysis of the commodity I do not stop at the double manner in which it is represented, but

---

3. Cf. Baudrillard, *Pour une critique de l'économie politique du signe* (Paris: Gallimard, 1972).

immediately go on to say that in this double being of
the commodity is represented *the two-fold character
of the labor* whose product it is: *useful labor*, i.e.,
the concrete modes of the labors which create use
values, and *abstract labor, labor as expenditure of
labor power*, irrespective of whatever 'useful' way it
is expended... that in the development of the *value
form of the commodity*, in the last instance of its
money form and hence of *money*, the *value* of a
commodity is represented in the *use value* of the
other, i.e., in the natural form of the other
commodity; that surplus value itself is derived from
a *'specific'* use value of labor power exclusively
pertaining to the latter, etc., etc., that thus for me
use value plays a far more important part than it has
in economics hitherto, however, that it is only ever
taken into account where this springs from the
analysis of a given economic constellations, not from
arguing backwards and forwards about the concepts
or words 'use value' and 'value' " (emphasis
added).[4]

In this passage it is clear that the use value of
labor, losing its "naturalness," takes on a
correspondingly greater "specific" value in the
structural functioning of exchange value. In
maintaining a kind of dialectical equilibrium
between concrete, qualitative labor and abstract,
quantitative labor, Marx gives logical priority to
exchange value (the given economic formation). But
in so doing, he retains something of the *apparent
movement of political economy*: the concrete
positivity of use value, a kind of concrete antecedent
within the structure of political economy. He does
not radicalize the schema to the point of reversing

---

4. "Notes on Wagner," in *Theoretical Practice* 5 (Spring,
1972), pp. 51-52.

this appearance and revealing use value *as produced by the play of exchange value*. We have shown this regarding the products of consumption; it is the same for labor power. The definition of products as useful and as responding to needs is the most accomplished, most internalized expression of abstract economic exchange: it is its subjective closure. The definition of labor power as the source of "concrete" social wealth is the complete expression of the abstract manipulation of labor power: the truth of capital culminates in this "evidence" of man as producer of value. Such is the twist by which exchange value retrospectively originates and logically terminates in use value. In other words, the signified "use value" here is still a code effect, the final precipitate of the law of value. Hence it is not enough to analyze the operation of the quantitative abstraction of exchange value *starting from* use value, but it is also necessary to bring out the condition of the possibility of this operation: the production of the concept of the use value of labor power itself, of a specific rationality of productive man. Without this generic definition there is no political economy. In the last instance, this is the basis of political economy. This generic definition must be shattered in unmasking the "dialectic" of quantity and quality, behind which hides the definitive structural institution of the field of value.

The Concrete Aspect of Labor: The "Dialectic" of Quality and Quantity

"The quantitative aspect of labor could not emerge until it was universalized during the 18th century in Europe... Until then, the different forms of activity were not fully comparable...labor

appeared then as diverse qualities."[5] During the
historical epoch of the artisanal mode of production,
qualitative labor was differentiated in relation to its
process, to its product, and to the destination of the
product. In the subsequent capitalist mode of
production labor is analyzed under a double form:
"While labor which creates exchange values is
abstract, universal and *homogeneous*, labor which
produces use values is concrete and special and is
made up of an endless variety of kinds of labor
according to the way in which and the material to
which it is applied."[6] Here we rediscover the
moment of use value: concrete, differentiated, and
incommensurable. In contrast to the quantitative
measure of labor power, labor use value, remains
nothing more or less than a qualitative potentiality.
It is specified by its own end, by the material it works
on, or simply because it is the expenditure of energy
by a given subject at a given time. The use value of
labor power is the moment of its actualization, of
man's relation to his useful expenditure of effort.
Basically it is an act of (productive) *consumption*;
and in the general process, this moment retains all
its uniqueness. At this level labor power is
incommensurable.

There is, moreover, a profound enigma throughout the articulation of Marx's theory: how is surplus
value born? How can labor power, by definition
qualitative, generate a measurable actualization?
One would have to assume that the "dialectical"
opposition of quantity and quality expresses only an

5. Pierre Naville, *Le nouveau léviathan* (Paris: Riviàre,
1954), p. 371.
6. Marx, *Contribution to the Critique of Political Economy*
(New York: International Publishers, 1904), p. 33.

apparent movement.

In fact, the *effect* of quality and of incommensurability once again partakes of the *apparent* movement of political economy. What produces the universalization of labor in the eighteenth century and consequently reproduces it is not the reduction of concrete, qualitative labor by abstract, quantitative labor but, from the outset, the structural articulation of the two terms. Work is really universalized at the base of this "fork," not only as market value but as human value. Ideology always thus proceeds by a binary, structural scission, which works here to universalize the dimension of labor. By dividing (or redividing into the qualitative structural effect, a *code* effect), quantitative labor spreads throughout the field of possibility. Henceforth there can be only labor — qualitative or quantitative. The quantitative still signifies only the commensurability of all forms of labor in abstract value; the qualitative, under the pretext of incommensurability, goes much further. It sinigifes *the comparability of all human practice in terms of production and labor*. Or better: the abstract and formal universality of the commodity labor power is what supports the "concrete" universality of qualitative labor.

But this "concrete" is an abuse of the word. It seems opposed to the abstract at the base of the fork, but in fact the fork itself is what establishes the abstraction. The autonomization of labor is sealed in the play of the two — from the abstract to the concrete, from the qualitative to the quantitative, from the exchange value to the use value of labor. In this structuralized play of signifiers, the fetishism of labor and productivity crystallizes. 7

---

7.   There is a further great disjuncture through which the

And what is this concrete aspect of labor? Marx says: "The indifference as to the particular kind of labor implies the existence of a highly developed aggregate of different species of concrete labor, none of which is any longer the predominant one. So do the most general abstractions commonly arise only where there is the highest concrete development, where one feature appears to be jointly possessed by many, and to be common to all."[8] But if one type of labor no longer dominates all others, it is because labor itself dominates all other realms. Labor is substituted for all other forms of wealth and exchange. Indifference to determined labor corresponds to a much more total determination of social wealth by labor. And what is the conception of this social wealth placed entirely under the sign of labor, if not use value? The "richest concrete development" is the qualitative and quantitative multiplication of use values. "The greater the extent to which historic needs — needs created by production itself, social needs — needs which are themselves the offspring of social production and intercourse, are posited as *necessary*, the higher the level to which real wealth has become developed. Regarded *materially*, wealth consists only in the manifold variety of needs."   Is

---

critique of political economy is articulated: the split between the technical and the social division of labor, which is subject to the same analysis. Transfiguring the technical division as both sides of the social division, it thus preserves the fiction of an ideal distribution of labor, of a concrete "non-alienated" productivity; and it universalizes the technical mode or technical reason. Thus the dialectic of productive forces-relations of production: everywhere the "dialectical" contradiction ends up as a Moebius band. But meanwhile this contradiction has circumscribed and universalized the field of production.

8.   *Contribution to the Critique of Political Economy, op. cit.*, pp. 298-299.

9.   *Grundrisse*, trans. M. Nicolaus (London: Pelican, 1973),

this not the program of advanced capitalist society? Failing to conceive of a mode of social wealth other than that founded on labor and production, Marxism no longer furnishes in the long run a real alternative to capitalism. Assuming the generic schema of production and needs involves an incredible simplification of social exchange by the law of value. Viewed correctly, this fantastic proposition is both arbitrary and strange with respect to man's status in society. The analysis of all primitive or archaic organizations contradicts it, as does the feudal symbolic order and even that of our societies, since all perspectives opened up by the contradictions of the mode of production drive us hopelessly into political economy.

The dialectic of production only intensifies the abstractness and separation of political economy. This leads us to the radical questioning of Marxist theoretical discourse. When in the last instance Marx defines the dialectical relation of abstract-concrete as the relation between "scientific representation and real movement" (what Althusser will analyze precisely as the *production* of a theoretical object), this theoretical production, itself taken in the abstraction of the representation, apparently only redoubles its object (in this case, the logic and movement of political economy). Between the theory and the object—and this is valid not only for Marxism—there is, in effect, a dialectical relation, in the bad sense: they are locked into a speculative dead end.[10] It becomes impossible to think outside the form production or the form representation.

---

p. 527.

10. We will return to this reciprocal neutralization of the theory and the object when we deal with the relations between Marxist theory and the workers' movement.

Man's Double "Generic" Face.

In fact the use value of labor power does not exist any more than the use value of products or the autonomy of signified and referent. The same fiction reigns in the three orders of production, consumption, and signification. Exchange value is what makes the use value of products appear as its anthropological horizon. The exchange value of labor power is what makes its use value, the concrete origin and end of the act of labor, appear as its "generic" alibi. This is the logic of signifiers which produces the "evidence" of the "reality" of the signified and the referent. In every way, exchange value makes concrete production, concrete consumption, and concrete signification appear only in distorted, abstract forms. But it foments the concrete as its ideological ectoplasm, its phantasm of origin and transcendence [*dépassement*]. In this sense need, use value, and the referent "do not exist."[11] They are only concepts produced and projected into a generic dimension by the development of the very system of exchange value.

By the same token, the double potentiality of man as needs and labor power, this double "generic" face of universal man, is only man as produced by the system of political economy. And productivity is not primarily a generic dimension, a human and social kernel of all wealth to be extracted from the husk of capitalist relations of production (the eternal empiricist illusion). Instead, all this must be overturned to see that the abstract and generalized development of productivity (the developed form of political economy) is what makes the *concept of*

---

11.   This does not mean *that they have never existed*. Hence we have another paradox that we must return to later.

production itself appear as man's movement and generic end (or better, as the concept of man as producer).

In other words, the system of political economy does not produce only the individual as labor power that is sold and exchanged: it produces the very conception of labor power as the fundamental human potential. More deeply than in the fiction of the individual freely selling his labor power in the market, the system is rooted in the identification of the individual with his labor power and with his act of "transforming nature according to human ends." In a work, man is not only quantitatively exploited as a productive force by the *system* of capitalist political economy, but is also metaphysically overdetermined as a producer by the *code* of political economy.[12] In the last instance, the system rationalizes its power here. *And in this Marxism assists the cunning of capital. It convinces men that they are alienated by the sale of their labor power, thus censoring the much more radical hypothesis that they might be alienated as labor power, as the "inalienable" power of creating value by their labor.*

If on the one hand Marx is interested in the later fate of the labor power objectified in the production process as abstract social labor (labor as its exchange value), Marxist theory, on the other hand, never challenges human capacity of production (energetic, physical, and intellectual), this productive potential of every man in every society "of transforming his environment into ends useful for the individual or the society," this *Arbeitsvermögen*. Criticism and

---

12.   Similarly for nature: there is not only the exploitation of nature as a productive force, but overdetermination of nature as referent, as "objective" reality, by the code of political economy.

history are strangely arrested before this anthropological postulate: a curious fate for a Marxist concept.

The same fate has befallen the concept of need in its present operation (the consumption of use value). It presents the same characteristics as the concrete aspect of labor: uniqueness, differentiation, and incommensurability—in short, "quality." If the one can be defined as "a specific type of action that produces its own product," the other is also defined as "a specific kind of tendency (or other psychologistic motivation, since all of this is only bad psychology) seeking its own satisfaction." Need also "decomposes both matter and form...into infinitely varied types of consumption." In concrete labor man gives a useful, objective end to nature; in need he gives a useful, subjective end to products. Needs and labor are man's double potentiality or double generic quality. This is the same anthropological realm in which the concept of production is sketched as the "fundamental movement of human existence," as defining a rationality and a sociality appropriate for man. Moreover, the two are logically united in a kind of ultimate perspective: "In a higher stage of community society...work will not be simply a means of living but will become the prime, vital need itself."[13]

Radical in its *logical* analysis of capital, Marxist theory nonetheless maintains an *anthropological* consensus with the options of Western rationalism in its definitive form acquired in eighteenth century bourgeois thought. Science, technique, progress, history—in these ideas we have an entire civilization that comprehends itself as producing its own

---

13.   *1844 Manuscripts*. [I have not been able to locate this quotation. Translator's note]

development and takes its dialectical force toward completing humanity in terms of totality and happiness. Nor did Marx invent the concepts of genesis, development, and finality. He changed nothing basic: nothing regarding the *idea* of man *producing* himself in his infinite determination, and continually surpassing himself toward his own end.

Marx translated this concept into the logic of material production and the historical dialectic of modes of production. But differentiating modes of production renders unchallengeable the evidence of production as the determinant instance. It generalizes the economic mode of rationality over the entire expanse of human history, as the generic mode of human becoming. It circumscribes the entire history of man in a gigantic simulation model. It tries somehow to turn against the order of capital by using as an analytic instrument the most subtle ideological phantasm that capital has itself elaborated. Is this a "dialectical" reversal? Isn't the system pursuing *its* dialectic of universal reproduction here? If one hypothesizes *that there has never been and will never be anything but the single mode of production ruled by capitalist political economy*—a concept that makes sense only in relation to the economic formation that produced it (indeed, to the theory that analyzes this economic formation)—then even the "dialectical" generalization of this concept is merely the *ideological* universalization of this system's postulates.

Ethic of Labor; Esthetic of Play

This logic of material production, this dialectic of modes of production, always returns beyond history to a generic definition of man as a dialectical being; a notion intelligible only through the process of the objectification of nature. This position is heavy with consequences to the extent that, even through the vicissitudes of his history, man (whose history is also his "product") will be ruled by this clear and definitive reason, this dialectical scheme that acts as an implicit philosophy. Marx develops it in the *1844 Manuscripts*; Marcuse revives it in his critique of the economic concept of labor: "...labor is an ontological concept of human existence as such." He cites Lorenz von Stein: "Labor is...in every way the actualization of one's infinite determinations through the self-positing of the individual personality [in which the personality itself] makes the content of the external world its own and in this way forces the world to become a part of its own internal world."[14] Marx: "Labor is *man's coming-to-be for himself* within *externalization* or as *externalized* man...[that is], the *self-creation* and self-objectification [of man]."[15] And even in *Capital*: "So far therefore as labor is a creator of use-value, is useful labor, it is a necessary condition, independent of all forms of society, for the existence of the human race; it is an external nature-imposed necessity, without which there can be no material exchanges between man and nature, and therefore no life."[16] "Labor is, in the first place, a process in which both man and nature participate, and in which man of his own accord starts, regulates, and controls the material re-actions between himself and nature. He

---

14. "On the Concept of Labor," *Telos* 16 (Summer, 1973), pp. 11-12.

15. Easton and Guddat, eds., *Writings of the Young Marx on Philosophy and Society* (New York: Anchor, 1969), pp. 322 and 332.

16. *Capital* (Moscow: Foreign Languages Publishing House), Vol. I, pp. 42-43.

opposes himself to nature as one of her own forces, setting in motion arms and legs, head and hands, the natural forces of his body, in order to appropriate nature's productions in a form adapted to his own wants."[17] The dialectical culmination of all of this is the concept of nature as "the inorganic body of man:" the naturalization of man and the humanization of nature.[18]

On this dialectical base, Marxist philosophy unfolds in two directions: an ethic of labor and an esthetic of non-labor. The former traverses all bourgeois and socialist ideology. It exalts labor as value, as end in itself, as categorical imperative. Labor loses its negativity and is raised to an absolute value. But is the "materialist" thesis of man's generic productivity very far from this "idealist" sanctification of labor? In any case, it is dangerously vulnerable to this charge. In the same article, Marcuse says: "...insofar as they take the concept of 'needs' and its satisfaction in the world of goods as the starting point, all economic theories fail to recognize the full factual content of labor.... The essential factual content of labor is not grounded in the scarcity of goods, nor in a discontinuity between the world of disposable and utilizable goods and human needs, but, on the contrary, in an essential excess of human existence beyond every possible situation in which it finds itself and the world."[19] On this basis he separates off play as a secondary activity: "In the structural sense, within the totality of human existence, labor is necessarily and

17.   *Ibid.*, p. 177.
18.   Engels, always a naturalist, goes so far as to exalt the role played by work in the transition from ape to man.
19.   Marcuse, *op.cit.*, p. 22.

eternally 'earlier' than play: it is the starting point, foundation, and principle of play insofar as play is precisely a breaking off *from* labor and a recuperation *for* labor."[20] Thus, labor alone founds the world as objective and man as historical. In short, labor alone founds a real dialectic of transcendence [*dépassement*] and fulfillment. Even metaphysically, it justifies the painful character of labor. "In the last analysis, the burdensome character of labor expresses nothing other than a negativity rooted in the very essence of human existence: man can achieve his own self only by passing through otherness: by passing through 'externalization' and 'alienation'."[21] I cite this long passage only to show how the Marxist dialectic can lead to the purest Christian ethic. (Or its opposite. Today there is a widespread contamination of the two positions on the basis of this transcendence of alienation and this intra-worldly asceticism of effort and overcoming where Weber located the radical germ of the capitalist spirit.) I have cited it also because this aberrant sanctification of work has been the secret vice of Marxist political and economic strategy from the beginning. It was violently attacked by Benjamin: "Nothing was more corrupting for the German workers' movement than the feeling of swimming with the current. It mistook technical development for the current, the direction it believed it was swimming in. From there, there was only one step to take in order to imagine that industrial labor represented a political performance. With German workers the old Protestant ethic of work celebrated, in a secular form, its resurrection.

---

20.   *Ibid.,* p. 15.
21.   *Ibid.,* p. 25.

The Gotha Program bore traces of this confusion. It defined work as 'the source of all wealth and culture.' To which Marx, even worse, objected that man possesses only his labor power, etc. However, the confusion spread more and more: and Joseph Dietzgen announced, 'Work is the Messiah of the modern world. In the amelioration of labor resides the wealth that can now bring what no redeemer has succeeded in'."[22] Is this "vulgar" Marxism, as Benjamin believes? It is no less "vulgar" than the "strange delusion" Lafargue denounced in *The Right to Be Lazy:* "A strange delusion possesses the working classes of the nations where capitalist civilization holds its sway."[23] Apparently, "pure and uncompromising" Marxism itself preaches the liberation of productive forces under the auspices of the *negativity* of labor. But, confronted by the "vulgar" idealism of the gospel of work, isn't this an "aristocratic" idealism? The former is positivist and the latter calls itself "dialectical." But they share the hypothesis of man's productive vocation. If we admit that it raises anew the purest metaphysics,[24] then the only difference between "vulgar" Marxism and the "other" Marxism would be that between a religion of the masses and a philosophical theory—not a great deal of difference.

Confronted by the *absolute* idealism of labor, dialectical materialism is perhaps only a *dialectical* idealism of productive forces. We will return to this

---

22. Walter Benjamin, *Poésie et révolution* (Paris: Denoël, 1971), p. 283.

23. Paul Lafargue, *The Right to Be Lazy*, trans. C. Kerr (Chicago: Kerr, 1917), p. 9.

24. Such as conceiving man as the union of a soul and a body —which gave rise to an extraordinary "dialectical" efflorescence in the Christian Middle Ages.

to see if the dialectic of means and end at the heart
of the principle of the transformation of nature does
not already virtually imply the autonomization of
means (the autonomization of science, technology,
and labor; the autonomization of production as
generic activity; the autonomization of the dialectic
itself as the general scheme of development).[25]

The regressive character of this work ethic is
evidently related to what it represses: Marx's chief
discovery regarding the double nature of labor (his
discovery of abstract and measurable social labor).
In the fine points of Marxist thought, confronting
the work ethic is an esthetic of non-work or play itself
based on the dialectic of quantity and quality.
Beyond the capitalist mode of production and the
quantitative measure of labor, this is the perspective
of a definitive qualitative mutation in communist
society: the end of alienated labor and the free
objectification of man's own powers. "In fact, the
realm of freedom actually begins only where labor
which is determined by necessity and mundane con-
siderations ceases; thus in the very nature of things it
lies beyond the sphere of actual material production.
...Freedom in this field can only consist in
socialized man, the associated producers, rationally
regulating their interchange with Nature, bringing
it under their common control, instead of being
ruled by it as by the blind forces of Nature; and
achieving this with the least expenditure of energy
and under conditions most favorable to, and worthy
of, their human nature. But it nonetheless still
remains a realm of necessity. Beyond it begins that

_____

25. But this autonomization is the key which turns Marxism
toward Social Democracy, to its present revisionism, and to tis
total positivist decay (which includes bureaucratic Stalinism as
well as Social Democratic liberalism).

development of human energy which is an end in itself, the true realm of freedom which, however, can blossom forth only with this realm of necessity as its basis."[26] Even Marcuse, who returns to the less puritanical (less Hegelian) conceptions, which, however, are totally philosophical (Schiller's esthetic philosophy), says that "Play and display, as principles of civilization, imply not the transformation of labor but its complete subordination to the freely evolving potentialities of man and nature. The ideas of play and display now reveal their full distance from the values of productiveness and performance. Play is *unproductive* and *useless* precisely because it cancels the repressive and exploitative traits of labor and leisure..."[27]

This realm beyond political economy called play, non-work, or non-alienated labor, is defined as the reign of a finality without end. In this sense it is and remains an *esthetic,* in the extremely Kantian sense, with all the bourgeois ideological connotations which that implies. Although Marx's thought settled accounts with bourgeois morality, it remains defenseless before its esthetic, whose ambiguity is more subtle but whose complicity with the general system of political economy is just as profound. Once again, at the heart of its strategy, in its analytic distinction between quantity and quality, Marxist thought inherits the esthetic and humanistic virus of bourgeois thought, since the concept of quality is burdened with all the finalities—whether those concrete finalities of use value, or those endless ideal and transcendent finalities. Here stands the defect of

---

26.   *Capital, op.cit.,* III, pp. 799-800.
27.   Marcuse, *Eros and Civilization* (New York: Vintage, 1962), p. 178.

all notions of play, freedom, transparence, or dis-
alienation: it is the defect of the *revolutionary
imagination* since, in the ideal types of play and the
free play of human faculties, we are still in a process
of repressive desublimation. In effect, the sphere of
play is defined as the fulfillment of human
rationality, the dialectical culmination of man's
activity of incessant objectification of nature and
control of his exchanges with it. It presupposes the
full development of productive forces; it "follows in
the footsteps" of the reality principle and the transformation of nature. Marx clearly states that it can
flourish only when founded on the reign of necessity.
Wishing itself beyond labor but *in its continuation*,
the sphere of play is always merely the esthetic
sublimation of labor's constraints. With this
concept we remain rooted in the problematic of
necessity and freedom, a typically bourgeois
problematic whose double ideological expression has
always been the institution of a reality principle
(repression and sublimation, the principle of labor)
and its formal overcoming in an ideal transcendence.

Work and non-work: here is a "revolutionary"
theme. It is undoubtedly the most subtle form of the
type of binary, structural opposition discussed
above. The end of the end of exploitation by work is
this reverse fascination with non-work, this reverse
mirage of free time (forced time-free time, full time-
empty time: another paradigm that fixes the
hegemony of a temporal order which is always
merely that of production). Non-work is still only the
repressive desublimation of labor power, the
antithesis which acts as the alternative. Such is the
sphere of non-work: even if it is not immediately
conflated with leisure and its present bureaucratic

organization, where the desire for death and mortification and its management by social institutions
are as powerful as in the sphere of work; even if it is
viewed in a radical way which *represents it* as other
than the mode of "total disposability" or "freedom"
for the individual to "produce" himself as value, to
"express himself," to "liberate himself" as a (conscious or unconscious) authentic *content*, in short, as
the ideality of time and of the individual as an empty
form to be filled finally by his freedom. The finality
of value is always there. It is no longer inscribed in
determined contents as in the sphere of productive
activity; henceforth it is a *pure form*, though no less
determining. Exactly as the pure institutional form
of painting, art, and theater shines forth in anti-
painting, anti-art, and anti-theater, which are
emptied of their contents, the pure form of labor
shines forth in non-labor. Although the concept of
non-labor can thus be fantasized as the abolition of
political economy, it is bound to fall back into the
sphere of political economy as the sign, and only the
sign, of its abolition. It already escapes revolutionaries to enter into the programmatic field of the
"new society."

Marx and the Hieroglyph of Value

Julia Kristeva writes in *Semiotica:* "From the
viewpoint of social distribution and consumption (of
communication), labor is always a value of use or
exchange... Labor is measurable according to the
value which it is, and not in any other way. Value is
measured by the quantity of time socially necessary
for production. But Marx clearly outlined another
possibility: *work could be apprehended outside
value*, on the side of the commodity produced and
circulating in the chain of communication. Here

labor no longer represents any value, meaning, or signification. It is a question only of a *body* and a *discharge* . . ."28

Marx writes, "The use values, coat, linen, etc., i.e., the bodies of commodities, are combinations of two elements—matter and labor. . . We see, then, that labor is not the only source of material wealth, of use-values produced by labor, as William Petty puts it, labor is its father and the earth its mother . . . Productive activity, if we leave out of sight its special form, viz., the useful character of the labor, is nothing but the expenditure of human labor-power."29

Is there a conception of labor in Marx different from that of the production of useful ends (the canonical definition of labor as value in the framework of political economy and the anthropological definition of labor as human finality)? Kristeva attributes to Marx a radically different vision centered on the body, discharge, play, anti-value, non-utility, non-finality, etc. She would have him read Bataille before he wrote—but also forget him when it is convenient. If there was one thing Marx did not think about, it was discharge, waste, sacrifice, prodigality, play, and symbolism. Marx thought about *production* (not a bad thing), and he thought of it in terms of value.

There is no way of getting around this. Marxist labor is defined in the absolute order of a natural necessity and its dialectical overcoming as rational activity producing value. The social wealth produced is *material*; it has nothing to do with

28. Julia Kristeva, "La sémiotique et la production," *Semiotica* 2. [I have not been able to complete this reference. Translator's note]

29. *Capital, op.cit.,* I, pp. 43-44.

symbolic wealth which, mocking natural necessity, comes conversely from destruction, the deconstruction of value, transgression, or discharge. These two notions of wealth are irreconcilable, perhaps even mutually exclusive; it is useless to attempt acrobatic transfers. According to Bataille, "sacrificial economy or symbolic exchange is exclusive of political economy (and of its critique, which is only its completion). But this is just to render to political economy what belongs to it: the concept of labor is consubstantial with it and therefore cannot be switched to any other analytical field. Above all, it cannot become the object of a science that pretends to surpass political economy. "The labor of the sign," "productive inter-textual space," etc., are thus ambiguous metaphors. There is a choice to be made between value and non-value. Labor is definitely within the sphere of value. This is why Marx's concept of labor (like that of production, productive force, etc.) must be submitted to a radical critique as an *ideological* concept. Thus, with all its ambiguities, this is not the time to generalize it as a *revolutionary* concept.

The quotations from Marx to which Kristeva refers do not at all carry the meaning she gives them. The genesis of wealth by the genital combination of labor-father and earth-mother certainly reinstates a "normal" productive reproductive scheme—one makes love to have children but not for pleasure. The metaphor is that of genital, reproductive sexuality, not of a discharge of the body in enjoyment! But this is only a trifle. The "discharge" of human power Marx speaks of is not a discharge with a pure waste, a symbolic discharge in Bataille's sense (pulsating, libidinal): it is still an economic, productive, finalized discharge precisely because, in its mating with the other, it begets a productive force called the earth (or matter). It is a useful discharge, an investment, not a gratuitous and festive energizing of the body's powers, a game with death, or the acting out of a desire. Moreover, this "discharge of the body" does not, as in play (sexual or otherwise), have its response in other bodies, its echo in a nature that plays and discharges in exchange. It does not establish a symbolic exchange. What man gives of his body in labor is never *given* or *lost* or *rendered* by nature in a reciprocal way. Labor only aims to "make" nature "yield." This discharge is thus immediately an investment of value, a *putting into value* opposed to all symbolic *putting into play* as in the gift or the discharge.

Kristeva poses the problem of redefining labor beyond value. In fact, as Goux has shown, for Marx the demarcation line of value cuts between use value and exchange value. "If we proceed further, and compare the process of producing value with the labor-process, pure and simple, we find that the latter consists of the useful labor, the work, that produces use-values. Here we contemplate the labor as producing a particular article; we view it under its qualitative aspect alone, with regard to its end and aim. But viewed as a value creating process, the same labor-process presents itself under its quantitative aspect alone. Here it is a question merely of the time occupied by the laborer in doing the work; — of the period during which the labor-power is usefully expended."[30] Hence the abstraction of value begins only in the second stage of exchange value. Thus use value is separated from the sphere of the production of value: or the realm

---

30. *Ibid.*, I, p. 195.

beyond value is confounded with the sphere of use value (this is Goux's interpretation, in which he extends this proposition to the use value of the sign). As we have seen, this is a very serious idealization of the process of concrete, qualitative labor and, ultimately, a compromise with political economy to the extent that the entire theoretical investment and strategy crystallizes on this line of demarcation within the sphere of value, leaving the "external" line of closure of this sphere of political economy in the shadows. By positing use value as the realm beyond exchange value, all transcendence is locked into this single alternative within the field of value. Qualitative production is already the realm of rational, positive finality; the transformation of nature is the occasion of its objectification as a productive force under the sign of utility (the same is true simultaneously of human labor). Even before the stage of exchange value and the equivalence through time of abstract social labor, labor and production constitute an abstraction, a reduction, and an extraordinary rationalization in relation to the richness of symbolic exchange. This "concrete" labor carries all the values of repression, sublimation, objective finality, "conformity to an end," and rational domestication of sexuality and nature. In relation to symbolic exchange, this *productive Eros* represents the real rupture which Marx displaces and situates between abstract quantitative labor and concrete qualitative labor. The process of "valorization" begins with the process of the useful transformation of nature, the instauration of labor as generic finality, and the stage of use value. The real rupture is not between "abstract" labor and "concrete" labor, but between symbolic exchange and work (production, economics). The abstract

social form of labor and exchange is only the
completed form, overdetermined by capitalist
political economy, of a scheme of rational valorization and production inaugurated long before
which breaks with every symbolic organization of
exchange.[31]

Kristeva would gladly be rid of value, but neither
labor nor Marx. One must choose. Labor is defined
(anthropologically and historically) as what disin-
vests the body and social exchange of all ambivalent
and symbolic qualities, reducing them to a rational,
positive, unilateral investment. The productive Eros
represses all the alternative qualities of meaning and
exchange in symbolic discharge toward a process of
production, accumulation, and appropriation. In
order to question the process which submits us to the
destiny of political economy and the terrorism of
value, and to rethink discharge and symbolic
exchange, the concepts of production and labor
developed by Marx (not to mention political
economy) must be resolved and analyzed as

---

31. For example, look at this passage from Marx on the
social hieroglyph: "Value, therefore, does not stalk about with a
label describing what it is. It is value, rather, that converts every
product into a social hieroglyphic. Later one, we try to decipher
the hieroglyphic, to get behind the secret of our own social
products; for to stamp an object of utility as a value, is just as
much a social product as language" (*Capital, op.cit.*, I, p. 74).
This entire analysis of the mystery of value remains
fundamental. But rather than being valid only for the product of
labor in distribution and exchange, it is valud even for the
product of labor (and for labor itself) taken as a "useful object."
Utility (including labor's) is already a socially produced and
determined hieroglyphic abstraction. The whole anthropology
of "primitive" exchange compels us to break with the natural
evidence of utility and to reconceive the social and historical
genesis of use value as Marx did with exchange value. Only then
will the hieroglyph be totally deciphered and the spell of value
radically exorcized.

ideological concepts interconnected with the general system of value. And in order to find a realm beyond economic value (which is in fact the only revolutionary perspective), then the *mirror of production* in which all Western metaphysics is reflected, must be broken.

Epistemology I:

In the Shadow of Marxist Concepts

Historical materialism, dialectics, modes of production, labor power — through these concepts Marxist theory has sought to shatter the abstract universality of the concepts of bourgeois thought (Nature and Progress, Man and Reason, formal Logic, Work, Exchange, etc.). Yet Marxism in turn universalizes them with a "critical" imperialism as ferocious as the other's.

The proposition that a concept is not merely an interpretive hypothesis but a translation of universal movement depends upon pure metaphysics. Marxist concepts do not escape this lapse. Thus, to be logical, the concept of history must itself be regarded as historical, turn back upon itself, and only illuminate the context that produced it by abolishing itself. Instead, in Marxism history is transhistoricized: it redoubles on itself and thus is universalized. To be rigorous the dialectic must dialectically surpass and annul itself. By radicalizing the concepts of production and mode of production at a given moment, Marx made a break in the social mystery of exchange value. The concept thus takes all its strategic power from its irruption, by which it dispossesses political economy of its imaginary universality. But, from the time of Marx, it lost this advantage when taken as a principle of explication.

It thus cancelled its "difference" by universalizing itself, regressing to the dominant form of the code (universality) and to the strategy of political economy. It is not tautological that the concept of history is historical, that the concept of dialectic is dialectical, and that the concept of production is itself produced (that is, it is to be judged by a kind of self-analysis). Rather, this simply indicates the explosive, mortal, present form of critical concepts. As soon as they are constituted as universal they cease to be analytical and the religion of meaning begins. They become canonical and enter the general system's mode of theoretical representation. Not accidentally, at this moment they also take on their scientific cast (as in the scientific canonization of concepts from Engels to Althusser). They set themselves up as expressing an "objective reality." They become signs: signifiers of a "real" signified. And although at the best of times these concepts have been practiced as concepts without taking themselves for reality, they have nonetheless subsequently fallen into the *imaginary of the sign*, or the *sphere of truth*. They are no longer in the sphere of interpretation but enter that of *repressive simulation*.

From this point on they only evoke themselves in an indefinite metonymic process which goes as follows: man is historical; history is dialectical; the dialectic is the process of (material) production; production is the very movement of human existence; history is the history of modes of production, etc. This scientific and universalist discourse (code) immediately becomes imperialistic. All possible societies are called on to respond. That is, consult Marxist thought to see if societies "without history" are something other than "pre"-historical, other than a chrysalis or larva. The dialectic of the world of production is not yet well developed, but nothing is lost by waiting—the Marxist egg is ready to hatch. Moreover, the psychoanalytic egg is in a similar condition. What we have said about the Marxist concepts holds for the unconscious, repression, Oedipal complex, etc., as well. Yet here, it is even better: the Bororos[32] are closer to primitive processes than we are.

This constitutes a most astonishing theoretical aberration—and a most reactionary one. There is *neither a mode of production nor production* in primitive societies. There is *no dialectic* and *no unconscious* in primitive societies. These concepts analyze only our own societies, which are ruled by political economy. Hence they have only a kind of boomerang value. If psychoanalysis speaks of the unconscious in primitive societies, we should ask about what represses psychoanalysis or about the repression that has produced psychoanalysis itself. When Marxism speaks of the mode of production in primitive societies, we ask to what extent this concept fails to account even for our own historical societies (the reason it is exported). And where all our ideologues seek to finalize and rationalize primitive societies according to their own concepts— to encode the primitives—we ask what obsession makes them see this finality, this rationality, and this code blowing up in their faces. Instead of exporting Marxism and psychoanalysis (not to mention bourgeois ideology, although at this level there is no difference), we bring all the force and questioning of primitive societies to bear on Marxism and psychoanalysis. Perhaps then we will break this fascination,

---

32. The Bororos are a South American society studied by Lévi-Strauss in *Tristes Tropiques*. [Translator's note]

this self-fetishization of Western thought. Perhaps
we will be finished with a Marxism that has become
more of a specialist in the impasses of capitalism
than in the roads to revolution, finished with a
psychoanalysis that has become more of a specialist
in the impasses of libidinal economy than in the
paths of desire.

The Critique of Political Economy
Is Basically Completed

Comprehending itself as a form of the rationality
of production superior to that of bourgeois political
economy, the weapon Marx created turns against
him and turns his theory into the dialectical apotheosis of political economy. At a much higher level, his
critique falters under his own objection to Feuerbach
of making a radical critique of the *contents* of
religion but in a completely religious *form*. Marx
made a radical critique of political economy, but
still in the form of political economy. These are the
ruses of the dialectic, undoubtedly the limit of all
"critique." The concept of critique emerged in the
West at the same time as political economy and, as
the quintessence of Enlightenment rationality, is
perhaps only the subtle, long-term expression of the
system's expanded reproduction. The dialectic does
not avoid the fate of every critique. Perhaps the
inversion of the idealist dialectic into a materialist
dialectic was only a metamorphosis; perhaps the
very logic of political economy, capital, and the
commodity is dialectical; and perhaps, under the
guise of producing its fatal internal contradiction,
Marx basically only rendered a descriptive theory.
The logic of representation — of the duplication of its
object — haunts all rational discursiveness. Every
critical theory is haunted by this surreptitious

religion, this desire bound up with the construction of its object, this negativity subtly haunted by the very form that it negates.

This is why Marx said that after Feuerbach the critique of religion was basically completed (cf. *Critique of Hegel's Philosophy of Right*) and that, to overcome the ambiguous limit beyond which it can no longer go (the reinversion of the religious form beneath the critique), it is necessary to move resolutely to a different level: precisely to the critique of political economy, which alone is radical and which can definitively resolve the problem of religion by bringing out the true contradictions. *Today we are exactly at the same point with respect to Marx.* For us, *the critique of political economy is basically completed.* The materialist dialectic has exhausted its content in reproducing its form. At this level, the situation is no longer that of a critique: it is inextricable. And following the same revolutionary movement as Marx did, we must move to a radically different level that, beyond its critique, permits the definitive resolution of political economy. This level is that of symbolic exchange and its theory. And just as Marx thought it necessary to clear the path to the critique of political economy with a critique of the philosophy of law, the preliminary to this radical change of terrain is the critique of the metaphysic of the signifier and the code, in all its current ideological extent. For lack of a better term, we call this the critique of the political economy of the sign.

II. MARXIST ANTHROPOLOGY AND
THE DOMINATION OF NATURE

In the 18th century, the simultaneous emergence of labor as the source of wealth and needs as the finality of produced wealth is captured at the zenith of Enlightenment philosophy in the appearance of the concept of Nature, around which gravitates the entire rationality of the system of political economy.

As late as the 17th century, Nature signified only the totality of laws founding the world's intelligebility: the guarantee of an order where men and things could exchange their meanings [*significations*]. In the end, this is God (Spinoza's "*Deus sive natura*"). Subject and world already have respective positions (as they had since the great Judeo-Christian rupture, to which we will return), but not in the sense of a mastery or exploitation of Nature, or conversely as the exaltation of an original myth. The rule for the autonomous subject confronting Nature is to form his practice so as to achieve an equilibrium of significations.

All this is shattered in the 18th century with the rise and "discovery" of Nature as a potentiality of *powers* (no longer a totality of *laws*); as a primordial source of life and reality lost and recovered, repressed and liberated; and as a deed projected into an atemporal past and an ideal future. This rise is only the obverse of an event: Nature's entry into the era of its technical domination. This is the definitive split between subject and Nature-object and their simultaneous submission to an operational finality. Nature appeared truly as an essence in all its glory but under the sign of the *principle of production*. This separation also involves the *principle of signification*. Under the objective stamp of Science, Technology, and Production, Nature becomes the great Signified, the great Referent. It is ideally charged with "reality"; it becomes *the* Reality, expressible by a process that is always somehow a process of labor, at once *transformation* and *transcription*. Its "reality" principle is this operational principle of an industrial structuration and a significative pattern.[1]

From the outset, this process rests on two separated terms whose separation, however, is complicitous: confronted by Nature "liberated" as a productive power, the individual finds himself "liberated" as labor power. Production subordinates Nature and the individual simultaneously as economic factors of production and as respective

---

1. This is why each product of labor will always be both a commodity and the *sign* of operable Nature and of its operation. In the framework of political economy, each product, besides its use value and exchange value, signifies and verifies the operationality of Nature and the "naturalness" of the process of production. This is why the commodity always has a value-sign, a coded value element. (It is not a question here of connotations of meaning that are grafted on during the stage of consumption. It is at the level of production itself that the commodity signifies, that it *represents* the principle of production and operationalization of Nature.) And, in the exchange of products, it is not only economic values but the code, this fundamental code, that circulates and is reproduced. Similarly, in the institution of labor power, man becomes not only economically operational but also the effect-referential of this operationality-sign.

terms of the same rationality—a transparency in which production is the mirror, directing articulation and expression in the form of a code.

For a long time, even in myth, production has been thought of in the mode of human reproduction. Marx himself spoke of labor as the father and the earth as the mother of produced wealth. This is false. In productive labor man does not make children with Nature. Labor is an objective transformation based on carving out and technically abstracting the subject and the object. Their relation is based only on the equivalence of the two terms as productive forces. What unifies them "dialectically" is the same abstract form.

Thus Nature gains force as ideal reference in terms of the very reality of its exploitation. Science presents itself as a project progressing toward an objective determined in advance by Nature. Science and Technology present themselves as revealing what is inscribed in Nature: not only its secrets but their deep purpose. Here the concept of Nature appears in all its ambiguity:

— It expresses only the finality of the domination of Nature inscribed in political economy. *Nature is the concept of a dominated essence* and nothing else. In this sense, it is Science and Technology that fulfill the essence of Nature by indefinitely reproducing it as separated.

— However, they do this in the name of a finality supposed to be Nature itself.

Hence the same concept operates in both cases: a factor of production and a model of finality; a servile, metaphorical instance of freedom; a detached, metaphorical instance of the totality. And it is by being sublimated and repressed that Nature becomes a metaphor of freedom and totality. Every-

thing that speaks in terms of totality (and-or
"alienation") under the sign of a Nature or a recovered essence speaks in terms of repression and
separation. Everything that invokes Nature invokes
the domination of Nature.

The Moral Philosophy of the Enlightenment

All the major concepts (those worthy of a capital
letter) depend on the same operation. The "People,"
for example, whose ideal reference emerges with the
collapse of traditional community and the urban
concentration of destructured masses. Marxist
analysis unmasked the myth of the People and
revealed what it ideally hides: wage earners and the
class struggle. On the other hand, Marxism only
partially dislocated the myth of Nature and the
idealist anthropology it supports. Marx indeed
"denaturalized" private property, the mechanisms of
competition and the market, and the processes of
labor and capital; but he failed to question the
following naturalist propositions:
— the useful finality of products as a function of
needs;
— the useful finality of nature as a function of its
transformation by labor.

The functionality of Nature structured by labor,
and the corresponding functionality of the subject
structured around needs, belong to the anthropological sphere of use value described by Enlightenment
rationality and defined for a whole civilization
(which imposed it on others) by a certain kind of abstract, linear, irreversible finality: a certain model
subsequently extended to all sectors of individual
and social practice.

This operational finality is arbitrary in such a way
that the concept of Nature it forgets resists inte-

gration within it. It looks as if forcefully rationalized Nature reemerges elsewhere in an irrational form. Without ceasing to be ideological, the concept splits into a "good" Nature that is dominated and rationalized (which acts as the ideal cultural reference) and a "bad" Nature that is hostile, menacing, catastrophic, or polluted. All bourgeois ideology divides between these two poles.

The same split occurs simultaneously at the level of man, through his idealist simplification as an element of the economic system. Starting with the 18th century, the idea of Man divides into a naturally good man (a projection of man sublimated as a productive force) and an instinctively evil man endowed with evil powers. The entire philosophical debate is organized around these sham alternatives, which result simply from the elevation of man to an economic abstraction. Marxism and all revolutionary perspectives are aligned on the optimist vision. They preserve the idea of an innate human rationality, a positive potentiality that must be liberated, even in the latest Freudo-Marxist version in which the unconscious itself is reinterpreted as "natural" wealth, a hidden positivity that will burst forth in the revolutionary act.

This dichotomy also occurs at the level of labor power. When exploited, labor power is good: it is within Nature and is normal. But, once liberated, it becomes menacing in the form of the proletariat. This contradiction is averted by assimilating the proletariat to a demonic, perverse, destructive Nature. Thus the dichotomy in the idea of Nature which expresses the profound separation in the economic order is admirably recuperated at the ideological level as a principle of moral order and social discrimination.

Fetishized for better or for worse, such is the true "alienation" of Nature and of the corresponding idea of Man. When at the same time he brands Nature and himself with the seal of production, man proscribes every relation of symbolic exchange between himself and Nature. It is this proscribed ambivalence that reemerges in the ambiguity of Nature and in man's own moral contradiction.

Marxism has not disencumbered itself of the moral philosophy of the Enlightenment. It has rejected its naive and sentimental side (Rousseau and Bernardin de Saint-Pierre), its cloying and fantastic religiosity (from the noble savage and the Age of Gold to the sorcerer's apprentice), but it holds onto the religion: the moralizing phantasm of a Nature to be conquered. By secularizing it in the economic concept of scarcity, Marxism keeps the idea of Necessity without transforming it. The idea of "natural Necessity" is only a *moral* idea dictated by political economy, the ethical and philosophical version of that bad Nature systematically connected with the arbitrary postulate of the economic. In the mirror of the economic, Nature looks at us with the eyes of necessity.

Marx says, "Just as the savage must wrestle with Nature to satisfy his wants, to maintain and reproduce life, so must civilized man, and he must do so in all social formations and under all possible modes of production. With his development this realm of physical necessity expands as a result of his wants: but, at the same time, the forces in production which satisfy these wants also increase."[2] What is not recognized here — and what allies Marx with the foundations of political economy — is that in

_____

2.   *Capital, op.cit.*, III, pp. 799-800.

his symbolic exchanges primitive man *does not guage himself in relation to Nature*. He is not aware of Necessity, a Law that takes effect only with the objectification of Nature. The Law takes its definitive form in capitalist political economy; moreover, it is only the philosophical expression of Scarcity. Scarcity, which itself arises in the market economy, is not a *given* dimension of the economy. Rather, it is what *produces and reproduces* economic exchange. In that regard it is different from primitive exchange, which knows nothing of this "Law of Nature" that pretends to be the ontological dimension of man.[3] Hence it is an extremely serious problem that Marxist thought retains these key concepts which depend on the metaphysics of the market economy in general and on modern capitalist ideology in particular. Not analyzed or unmasked (but exported to primitive society where they do not apply), these concepts mortgage all further analysis. The concept of production is never questioned; it will never radically overcome the influence of political economy. Even Marxism's transcending perspective will always be burdened by counter-dependence on political economy. Against Necessity it will oppose the mastery of Nature; against Scarcity it will oppose Abundance ("to each according to his needs") without ever resolving either the arbitrariness of these concepts or their idealist overdetermination by political economy.

The political order is at stake here. Can the quantitative development of productive forces lead to a revolution of social relations? Revolutionary hope is

---

3. Cf. Marshall Sahlins, "La première société d'abondance," *Les Temps Modernes* (October, 1968), pp. 641-680.

based "objectively" and hopelessly on this claim. Even for Marcuse in *The End of Utopia*, the due date of revolution is at hand given our technological potentials: quantitative change is possible as of now. Even when the situation has clearly drifted enormously far from revolution and the dominant social relations support the very development of productive forces in an endless spiral, this dialectical voluntarism, for which Necessity exists and must be conquered, is not shaken. Scarcity exists and must be abolished; the Productive Forces exist and must be liberated; the End exists and only the means need be found. All revolutionary hope is thus bound up in a Promethean myth of productive forces, but this myth is only the space time of political economy. And the desire to manipulate destiny through the development of productive forces plunges one into the space time of political economy. The wish to abolish scarcity is not furthered by restoring an integrated productivity. The *concept* of Scarcity itself, the concept of Necessity, and the concept of Production must be exploded because they rivet the bolt of political economy. No dialectic leads beyond political economy because it is the very movement of political economy that is dialectical.

Lycurgus and Castration

Parallel to the concepts of Necessity, Scarcity, and Need in the (vulgar or dialectical) materialist code, the psychoanalytic concepts of Law, Prohibition, and Repression are also rooted in the objectification of Nature.

Vernant cites the story of Lycurgus.[4] Lycurgus

---

4. *Mythe et pensée chez les Grecs* (Paris: Maspero, 1966), p. 205.

kills his son Dryas or, in other versions, cuts off his foot believing he is trimming a vine. In another story, Phylacus makes his son impotent while trimming a tree or butchering livestock. Hence the violence against nature (the rupture of exchange with and symbolic obligation toward it) is immediately expiated. All the myths of a vengeful, bad, *castrating* nature take root here. And this is no mere metaphor, as the story clearly indicates. The rupture is immediately the foundation of *castration*, of the Oedipus complex (in this case parental, since the father emasculates the son), and of Law. For only then does Nature appear as an implacable necessity, "the alienation of man's own body." Marx adopted this Law of Necessity along with the Promethean and Faustian vision of its perpetual transcendence, just as psychoanalysis adopted the principle of castration and repression, prohibition and law (in the Lacanian version, by inscription in the order of the Signifier). But in no sense is it a fundamental structure. Neither Law nor Necessity exist at the level of reciprocity and symbolic exchange, where the break with nature that leads to the irreversibility of castration — and consequently to the entire becoming of history (the operational violence of man against nature) and of the unconscious (the redemption of the symbolic debt owed for this operational violence) — has not occurred. In this sense law, which is called the foundation of the symbolic order and of exchange, results instead from the rupture of exchange and the loss of the symbolic. This is why there is properly neither Necessity nor Scarcity nor Repression nor the Unconscious in the primitive order, whose entire symbolic strategy aims at exorcizing the apparition of Law.[5]

5.　And the incest taboo? Already this all-powerful concept

Under the sign of Necessity and Law, the same fate — sublimation — awaits Marxism and psychoanalysis. We have seen how materialism's reference to "objective" Necessity led it to fantasize in its revolutionary perspectives the reverse schemes of Freedom and Abundance (the universality of needs and capacities) which are only the sublimated counterparts of Law and Necessity. Similarly, the analytic reference to the Unconscious, product of repression and prohibition, leads to the same step (today psychoanalysis is being short-circuited on a very large scale, and this turning away cannot be called accidental): an ideal reference to a "liberation" of the Unconscious and to its universalization by removing repression.[6] In this case as well, an ideal-revolutionary sublimation of a *content* results from accepting an essential *form* given as irreducible. But this form is merely the specific abstraction of an order that has cancelled symbolic relation in favor of operational violence, symbolic exchange in favor of

---

has lost its legitimacy. Cf. Deleuze and Guattari, *Capitalisme et schizophrénie: L'Anti-Oedipe* (Paris: Minuit, 1972), and also d'Oritgues, *L'Oedipe africain* (Paris: Plon, 1966), etc.

6.   That is, to the universalization of a positivized libido and Eros that are "liberated" as value, by which revolutionaries rejoin all the culturalist neo-Freudians in an optimistic, moralizing vision. But the other, strictly Freudian perspective (normally connoting "pessimism") is based on the economic interpretation (the Nirvana principle and a resolution of tensions). Although this interpretation takes the problem of death into account, it contradicts all traditional humanism (idealist or revolutionary), resting instead on a conception of man in terms of instincts. This "materialist" vision is also moral and is secretly directed by Law, an instance of sublimation and repression, and hence the finality of a resolution of these instincts either in the transgression of this Law (the pleasure principle) or in repression (Nirvana principle). In neither case can a resolution of Law be envisioned.

the Law of castration and value—or, better, it has cancelled the actualization of the death impulse and the ambivalence in exchange in favor of a productive Eros split into a symbolic violence of the Unconscious.

Judaeo-Christian Anti-Physis

This separation from Nature under the sign of the principle of production is fully realized by the capitalist system of political economy, but obviously it does not emerge with political economy. The separation is rooted in the great Judaeo-Christian dissociation of the soul and Nature. God created man in his *image* and created Nature for man's *use*. The soul is the spiritual hinge by which man is God's image and is radically distinguished from the rest of Nature (and from his own body): "Uniquely in its Western form, Christianity is the most anthropocentric religion the world has ever known. In absolute contrast to ancient paganism and oriental religions, Christianity not only institutes a dualism of Man and Nature but also affirms that God's will is that man exploit Nature according to his own ends."[7]

Rationality begins here. It is the end of paganism, animism and the "magical" immersion of man in nature, all of which is reinterpreted as superstition. ("Rational" Marxism makes the same error by reinterpreting it in terms of the "rudimentary" development of productive forces.) Hence although science, technology, and material production subsequently enter into contradiction with the cultural order and the dogmas of Christianity, nonetheless their condition of possibility remains the Christian postulate of man's transcendence of

7. *Science* (Paris), March, 1967.

nature. This is why a scientific movement does not emerge in Greece. Greek rationality remains based on a conformity with nature radically distinguished from the Christian rationality and "freedom" based on the separation of man and nature and on the domination of nature.

This separation immediately establishes not a work ethic (of material domination and production) but an ethic of asceticism, suffering, and self-mortification: an "other-worldly" ethic of sublimation, in Max Weber's expression. Not a productive morality but a fixed order is outlined, in which well-being is to be "earned." And this is an *individualist* enterprise. The passage from the ascetic to the productive mode, from mortification to labor, and from the finality of welfare to the secularized finality of needs (with the Puritan transition at the origin of capitalism where work and rational calculation still have an ascetic, intra-worldly character and an orientation toward well-being) changes nothing in the principle of separation and sublimation, repression and operational violence. Well-being and labor are both well within the realm of ends and means. From ascetic practices to productive practices (and from the latter to consumer practices) there is thus *desublimation*; but the desublimation is only a metamorphosis of repressive sublimation. The ethical dimension is secularized under the sign of the material domination of nature.

Christianity is thus on the hinge of a rupture of symbolic exchanges. The ideological form most appropriate to sustain the intensive rational exploitation of nature[8] takes form within Christian-

---

8. Yet it was repeatedly intersected by contradictory, heretical currents, which in their protest were always attached to

ity during a long transition: from the 13-14th century when work begins to be imposed as value, up to the 16th century when work is organized around its rational and continuous scheme of value — the capitalist productive enterprise and the system of political economy, that secular generalization of the Christian axiom about nature. But this revolution of the rational calculus of production which Weber noted is not the beginning; it is prefigured in the Christian rupture. Political economy is only a kind of actualization of this break.

Epistemology II:

Structural Limits of the Marxist Critique

The above discussion poses a serious methodological question (which will arise again later in the discussion of the Marxist interpretation of earlier societies). Basing the intelligibility of the contradictions of political economy on the structural givens of the finished system (capital), Marxist analysis cannot

---

"naturism": a rehabilitation of nature, a beyond of Christianity most often expressed only by a nostalgia for the origins of Christianity. From St. Francis of Assisi with his Christ-like angelicism (all creatures praise God, etc.) — but St. Francis was a sort of fire fighter for the Catholic Church quenching the flames of the Cathar and pantheist heresies that threatened to engulf the whole Western world — to Spinoza with his subtle and impious pantheism (God is everywhere in Nature, thus he is nowhere) and all the Adamite sects that preached the refusal of labor and the resurrection of the body, and dreamt of abolishing the very finality of the Christian order (its principle of transcendence and sublimation) in their immediate demand for the end of the whole world and for "Paradise now." Against all these naturalist, pantheistic, mystical, libertarian and millenarian heresies, the Church always defended, along with the original break with nature, a morality of effort and merit, of labor and works, which was coupled with the evolution of the order of production and connected with the political dimension of power.

account for these basic coordinates of economic rationality—because the system of political economy tends to project itself retrospectively as a model and subordinates everything else to the genealogy of this model. When Marxism takes up its critique it does not question this retrospective finality. Thus in the strict sense, it analyzes only the conditions of the model's *reproduction*, of its production as such: of the separation that establishes it.[9] The analysis of the production of *the economic as finality and as universal principle of reality*, the analysis of the production of the *production principle*, escapes Marxism since it moves only within the structural field of production. By presupposing the axiom of the economic, the Marxist critique perhaps deciphers the *functioning* of the *system* of political economy; but at the same time it reproduces it as a model. By pretending to illuminate earlier societies in the light of the present structure of the capitalist economy, it fails to see that, abolishing their difference, it projects onto them the spectral light of political economy.

Marx affirmed that it is on the basis of a critical return to its own contradictions that (our) culture becomes capable of grasping earlier societies. Thus we must conclude—and thereby grasping the *relativity* of Marxist analysis—that in Marx's time

---

9.   Likewise, structural linguistics cannot account for the emergence of language as a *means of communication*: it can only analyze its functioning, and thus its reproduction, as such. But this destination of language, which linguistics takes as an axiom, is merely an extraordinary reduction of language (and hence of the "science" that analyzes it). And what operates in this "science," in the last instance, is the reproduction of this arbitrary model of language. Similarly, the structural analysis of capital only leads back to its principle of logical reality (in which "science" itself participates).

the system of political economy had not yet developed all its contradictions, hence that even for Marx radical critique was not yet possible nor was the real comprehension of earlier societies. Marx himself could not encroach on the system's total logic. Only at a certain stage of development and saturation of the system can critique go to its *roots*. In particular, the fundamental determinations of the economic (form production and form representation), the break they establish in relation to symbolic exchange, and the way a radical revolution of social relations is sketched starting from them can be read only after political economy has invaded all fields of social and individual practice, far beyond the field of material production. It is useless to question Marx about these matters. Analyzing one phase and only one phase of the general process, his critique goes only so far and can only be extrapolated regarding the remainder. Marxism is the projection of the class struggle and the mode of production onto all previous history; it is the vision of a future "freedom" based on the conscious domination of nature. These are extrapolations of the economic. To the degree that it is not *radical*, Marxist critique is led despite itself to reproduce the roots of the system of political economy.

III. HISTORICAL MATERIALISM
AND PRIMITIVE SOCIETIES

Having analyzed the rewriting of Nature according to the code of production, it is also necessary to analyze the *rewriting of History through the mode of production.* In fact, the two projects are intertwined since the crucial point of the "materialist" decipherment is societies "without history." Moreover, it is not a matter of rewriting but simply of writing. The schema of production does not reinterpret a nature present outside it; the schema of the mode of production does not reinterpret a history already there. Instead, the concepts of production and mode of production themselves "produce" and "reproduce" the concepts of Nature and History as their space time. The model produces this double horizon of extent and time: Nature is only its extent and History only its trajectory. They do not need somehow to have their own names because they are only emanations of the code, referential simulations that acquire the force of reality and behind which the code legislates. These are the "laws of Nature" and the "laws of History." A third instance recovers the other two: their apparent movement is to be read in the Dialectic, which also takes the force of law. These are the "laws of the Dialectic" that govern History (and indeed Nature, for Engels). All these concepts

are articulated under the sign of materialism in a
critical perspective, according to the *critical illusion*.
This is not a perspective in the Nietzschean sense,
which consists in deconstructing the imaginary universality of the solidest conceptual edifices (the
subject, rationality, knowledge, history, dialectics)
and restoring them to their relativity and
symptomality, piercing the truth *effect* by which
every system of interpretation doubles itself in the
imaginary: in short, by unmasking ideology — in the
present case, ideology under the materialist and
dialectical sign of production. The logos and the
pathos of production must be reduced according to
this radical perspectivism.

Structural Causality and the Primitives

Economic anthropology bears witness to the
impossibility of accounting for societies without
history, writing, or relations of production (one
wonders with horror how they could exist without
them). We will use as a reference Marxist
anthropological thought, specifically Godelier's in
"Sur les sociétés précapitalistes," and "L'anthropologie économique," in *L'anthropologie, science des
sociétés primitives?*[1]

With all its concepts, this thought tackles a
dangerous object and risks being analyzed in return
if it does not quickly master that object (all critical
analysis must aspire to this — but then what becomes
of science?). Hence the object must be approached
without dogmatism. "The causality of the economy
cannot be presented as the genesis of social
superstructures outside the bosom [!] of the
economic infrastructure."[2] "It is hard to see what

---

1.   (Paris: Denoël, 1971).
2.   *Ibid.* [I have not been able to locate the page references

secret alchemy can make the economy become
kinship, or for what mysterious reason the economic
could be (badly) hidden under kinship."3 (But who
forces Godelier to seek it there? Perhaps there is
nothing hidden at all, and he merely enjoys hide-
and-seek.) Does this doctrinal agility augur
lacerating revision of concepts? Hardly. Immediately, one reads: "Thus, the relations of kinship
function both as elements of the infrastructure and
as superstructure."4 What could this possibly mean?
The "mysterious" reason is clearly the will to
preserve the distinction between the infrastructure
and the superstructure; without which historical
materialism collapses. All the rest is only reformist
scrupulosity.

By an adjustment of the concept of mode of
production, Marxist anthropology thus seeks from
beginning to end to preserve materialist orthodoxy
against the heresy of primitive societies. "The
economist easily distinguishes the productive forces
in these societies that rest on hunting, fishing, etc.
The relations of production, on the contrary, do not
appear separated from social, political, religious or
kinship relations."5 Logically, if there are no longer
relations of production (since they are not definable
as such), there is no longer any mode of production.
And how can it be admitted that we can deal with
"productive forces" before any relations of production have hatched? This is hardly a Marxist position.
If the productive forces are only the emanation or
exercise of preexisting relations,6 there is no sense in

for any of the quotes from Godelier. Translator's note]
   3.   Ibid.
   4.   Ibid.
   5.   Ibid.
   6.   Cf. Sahlins, op.cit.

implanting this concept as such. Furthermore, the concept must "produce," come what may; the separation of productive forces and relations of production must be saved, relieved of keeping the relations of production on ice, if they are not still "to appear as separated." This facile cleverness saves the "dialectical" grid which establishes the economy as the determinant instance. But the only dialectic here is that of the reproduction fo the theory through the formal simulation of its object.

The theory results in a perfect sophism of recovery, undoubtedly the masterpiece of a structuralist materialism with "scientific" pretentions! "The fundamental task of economic anthropology is to analyze the role of the economy as *determinant in the last instance,* and, relative to the modes of production and the historical epochs, the dominant role of social structures which at the same time fix the non-economic functions."[7] Dominant? Determinant? What can this mean if not the remodeling of the infra-superstructure determinist causality into a more flexible causality allowing the retention of economic determinism? Clarifying this, moreover, Marx writes: "This much, however, is clear, that the middle ages could not live on Catholicism, nor the ancient world on politics. On the contrary, it is the mode in which they gained a livelihood that explains why here politics, and there Catholicism, played the chief part."[8] Finally (argues Godelier), no society can exist without economics; hence, economics is the determinant instance (if so, then many things can take the role of determinant instance: for example, language). In any case, here is the extreme

7. Godelier, *op.cit.*
8. *Capital, op.cit.*, I, p. 82n.

limit of the theoretical adjustment by which
Godelier risks showing how nothing essential has
changed: "Under certain conditions, kinship *is*
economy, and religion can function directly as a
relation of production."9 This is as much as saying
that he cannot imagine the primacy of anything
except through the primacy of the economy. And
certainly this is linked to the primacy of history: "As
soon as humanity exists [!], the functions of
economics, kinship, and ideology exist with a
determined content and form. This content and this
form are transformed with history and by it... In
sum, anthropology and history turn up as two
complementary fragments of the single science of
history."10 Godelier exhibits a theoretical mania for
fragmenting the object into functions in order then
to dialecticize them "historically"—in fact, to
structuralize them under the hegemony of one of
them—and to reconcile the whole under the sign of
science! All this is false. It is the paranoid idealist
projection of a rationalizing machine where all
concepts are mutually engendered according to an
apparent dialectical movement (production, economy, science, history) but in fact finalized by a
science which sees only separation and which, to be
fulfilled, projects an imaginary anthropology of
separated functions. Productivism, scientism, and
historicism all fashion for anthropology an object in
their own image, dislocated so that it responds to
their own theoretical manipulation.

In this regard Godelier innocently affirms that
"For reasons internal to his scientific practice, the
anthropologist must question the ideology that

---

9. Godelier, *op.cit.*
10. *Ibid.*

beleaguers the interior of his scientific practice."[11]
But what if this "scientific" practice by itself was
already this ideology? In that case there is no need
for interrogation. But the specificity of the
anthropological object is precisely the impossibility
of defining the economic and the mode of
production as a separated instance. The very least
requirement would thus be to reexamine the whole
matter *starting from this non-separation.* This is
impossible for a "science" that can only "dialectically" (to the hierarchical advantage of one instance)
synthesize its object, having carefully dismantled it.
No ideology is more profound than this one so
profound that it eludes Marxist-scientific good will.
The Copernican revolution has not yet occurred in
anthropology; and in its geocentric or egocentric
discourse bourgeois and Marxist Western thought
continues to describe the *apparent* movement of
primitive exchanges.

Surplus and Anti-Production

Everywhere Godelier's position is full of abrupt
postulations and ambiguous extrapolations. For
example, "One can say in general that in a primitive
society the producers control their means of
production and their own labor; that production is
oriented more toward the satisfaction of needs than
toward the search for a profit; that exchange, when
it exists, operates according to culturally determined
principles of equivalence between goods and services
which circulate among the partners of the
exchange."[12] There are no producers; there are no
"means of production" and no objective labor,

---

11.   *Ibid.*
12.   *Ibid.*

controlled or not. There are no needs and no satisfactions that orient them: this is the old illusion of subsistence economy! And exchange does not operate according to principles of equivalence, even "culturally determined" ones. The exchange-gift, to be exact, operates not according to the evaluation or equivalence of exchanged goods but according to the antagonistic reciprocity of persons. All this is more or less fraudulently exported from our political economy. Even if the intention is to nuance the structure and modalities of primitive "economy," the result is to inscribe it in the same discourse as ours: with the same code. It means looking at primtive society from the wrong end.

Consider the production of a surplus. There is ever-renewed amazement at the fact that primtives do not produce a surplus "whereas they could produce one"! It is impossible to think this non-growth, this non-productive desire. The West, as is logical with regard to its own assumptions, always thinks of it as an anomaly, a *refusal* to produce. If the primitives "produce," it is incomprehensible that they do not produce more (production implies the expanding reproduction of productive forces; the truth of production is productivity, a quantitative growth function). The solution must be that they produce "only for their needs." But this is to fall from Charybdis to Scylla, since needs themselves are an undefined function and it is completely arbitrary to arrest them at the threshold of a basic minimum of survival, which has no strict economic justification and derives directly from moral philosophy: from a distinct opposition we have reinvented starting from a moral conception of the superfluous and the artificial (and from the functionalist vision of the instinct for self-preservation). The savages are "nature." When they have "enough," they stop "producing." This formula contains both perplexed admiration and racist commiseration. Moreover, it is false. The savages fritter away their resources in feasts and risk living "beneath the basic minimum." And although he shows very well how in their festive exchanges the Siane pour back the extra that comes from contact with white civilization, Godelier persists in affirming that "in nearly every case, primitive societies produce a surplus but they do not."[13] Or better yet: "this surplus remains in a potential state"![14] "It seems that they have no reason to produce it." In fact, this concept makes no sense for them. How could reasons to produce a surplus occur to them? Only the anthropologist has good reasons to produce it so that he can discreetly impute it to the savages and then dejectedly verify their bewildering indifference in this regard. Subsistence plus surplus: only the presupposition of production permits this quantitative reduction to additional functions *neither of which* makes sense in primitive exchange.

Subsistence, basic minimum, needs—these are only some of the magical concepts to which the anthropologist has recourse in resolving the impossible economic equation of primitive societies. Other variables help correct the infrastructural equation: the "social," the "cultural," the "historical" (the same desperate patching-up as in our modernist neo-economics). "The simple correlation, at other times assumed, between the existence

---

13. *Ibid.*
14. Marx says: "By thus acting in the external world and changing it, he at the same time changes his own nature. He develops his slumbering powers and compels them to act in obedience to his sway" (*Capital, op.cit.,* I, p. 177).

of a surplus, leisure time, invention of culture [!], and the progress of civilization, today no longer appears to be based on the facts and demands a reinterpretation of the conditions of the evolution of social life and history." But this "correlation" demands nothing at all, especially not to be mended and corrected by categories derived from the same discourse. This totally artificial construct simply calls for being deconstructed into its terms. The conclusion would then be reversed. The infrastructure is not adequate. It can be mixed with the socio-cultural—but this is equally abstract since, strictly speaking, the socio-cultural specified as such designates only what is left over from the infrastructure. Godelier's mistake is wanting like Baron Münchhausen, to get out of the vessel by pulling himself up by the hair: "The productivity of labor is measured not only in technical terms...it depends even more on social conditions."[16] Hence, there is something "social" in primitive societies which prevents technology from developing and producing a surplus.[17] These acrobatics of the reduction of factors and the remixing "in the dominant" is only conceptual violence. We now know that it is even more destructive than missionaries or venereal disease.[18]

---

15. Godelier, *op.cit.*

16. *Ibid.*

17. It is useless to insist on the *political* consequences of this aberration. All neo-imperialist politics is inspired by it. Hence, it is necessary to "eliminate" these social and cultural obstacles in order to pave the way for "modern" technological growth.

18. The symbolic itself does not escape this structural reconstruction. Godelier says: "It is because kinship functions here directly, internally, as an economic, political, and ideological relation, that it functions as the *symbolic* form in which the content of social life is expressed, as the general language of men

Having contested the correlation between surplus and culture, Godelier quickly recaptures it for his account in a different form: "These economies do not limit themselves to the production of subsistence goods; they produce a surplus destined for the functioning of social structures (kinship, religion, etc.)."[19] These societies seem to be sustained according to manuals of modern economics: they obey the same rationality of choice, calculation, allocation of resources, etc. (an imagery that is, moreover, as false for our societies as for the primitives). Hence they subsist, and they then begin to exist "socially." Here again is the absurd attempt to make a separate function out of the "social." Primitive "society" does not exist as an instance apart from symbolic exchange; and this exchange never results from an "excess" of production. It is the opposite: to the extent that these terms apply here,

---

between themselves and with nature." The symbolic is thus conceived as a form expressing contents (as language, but according to the traditional linguistic vision). This allows Godelier to concede predominance to it (societies with "symbolic predominance" — Terray) without, however, renouncing the contents and separated functions which remain, under "symbolic" *expression*, the true instance of reference (the economic in particular) which is ready to emerge at the right moment "under the pressure of productive forces." "It is not kinship that is mysteriously transformed into political relations. It is the political function *present in the old relations of kinship* that is developed on the base of new problems." Here we have a new version as mysterious as the other but which resolves the problem by an appeal to principle.

Thus conceived, the symbolic mode, a correlative to others in the array of instances, is no longer at all opposed to the economic mode (one could say that primitive societies "produce" the symbolic as ours "produce" the economic). The symbolic is assigned a functional office and isolated as a category. It is assigned a structural position as a satellite term of the economic: in short, it is emptied of its meaning.

19.   Godelier, *op.cit*.

"subsistence" and "economic exchange" are the *residue* of symbolic exchange, a *remainder*. Symbolic circulation is primordial. Things of functional use are *taken from* that sphere (ultimately the substraction will be null and everything will be symbolically consumed). Nothing remains because survival is not a principle. *We* have made it one. For the primitives, eating, drinking, and living are first of all acts that are exchanged: if they are not exchanged, they do not occur.

But the "residual" is still too arithmetic. In fact, there is a certain type of exchange, symbolic exchange, where the relation (not the "social") is tied, and *this exchange excludes any surplus:* anything that cannot be exchanged or symbolically shared would break the reciprocity and institute power. Better yet, *this exchange excludes all "production."* The exchanged goods are apportioned and limited, often imported from far away according to strict rules. Why? Because, given over to individual or group production, they would risk being proliferated and thereby break the fragile mechanism of reciprocity. Godelier says that "Everything happens as if primitive societies had instituted *scarcity.*"20 But this "scarcity" is not the quantitative, restrictive scarcity of a market economy: it is neither privative nor antithetical to "abundance." It is the condition of symbolic exchange and circulation. It is not the socio-cultural realm that limits "potential" production; instead, exchange itself is based on non-production, eventual destruction, and a process of continuous *unlimited* reciprocity between *persons*, and inversely on a strict

20. *Ibid.*

limitation of exchanged *goods*. It is the exact opposite of our economy based on unlimited production of goods and on the discontinuous abstraction of contractual exchange. In primitive exchange, production appears nowhere as an end or a means: the meaning occurs elsewhere. It is not there as (even underlying) potential. On the contrary, in its accumulative finality and its rational autonomy (production is always end and means), it is continually negated and volatilized by reciprocal exchange which consumes itself in an endless operation.

Godelier ignores all this and colors the objects of exchange with his schema. "At first they function [note the obsession with functionality!] as commodities; then, at the interior [?], as objects of gift and prestige... The same object thus changes function, but the second of these two functions is dominant."[21] (Implication: the first function is determinant!) Thus, the code of Marxist anthropology is saved by multi-functional superimposition! From here one can easily go on to disentangle by simple decantation our own historical stage (we have never left it), in which political economy (and with it its materialist critique) is finally able to recognize what is its own. "Thus one understands better why, from Antiquity to our own day, these objects are stripped more and more of their dominant trait as objects to be given, and why they become specialized in the dominant mode of commercial objects while preserving a traditional aspect."[22] The term "stripped" indicates the profound theoretical racism of these categorizations, which intend only to produce in the course of history what these objects

---

21. *Ibid.*
22. *Ibid.*

already were in the matrix of an archaic economy without being known as such—what historical materialism makes them into: objects of production. For all these objects and men lost in their primitive limbo, this is the *baptism of production*: the baptism of labor and value for nature and goods lost in the gratuity of their richness; the baptism of the economic, of the mode of production, and of the determinant instance for all these exchanges that knew neither instance, determination, nor economic rationality. The materialist missionaries have arrived.

Magic and Labor

The same blind determinism-in-several-instances leads to the same kind of incomprehension of magic: "For primitive man, labor is experienced and thought as the interior and indivisible unity of magic and technical knowledge."[23] In other words, the Trobrianders "know" that it is necessary to work in their gardens, but they think that this work is not enough and that magic is indispensable in order to guarantee the harvest. Magic is basically only insurance on the productive forces of nature! "By his magical practices, man thinks he can insert himself in the natural order's chain of necessary causalities."[24] In nature he sees forces "that he spontaneously endows with human attributes." He conceives of it "by analogy with society, as a network of intentional relations" where the rituals and magical practices were designed to underhandedly influence these forces, etc. This vulgar rewriting of magic is always dominated by the prejudice of a separated

---

23.   *Ibid.*
24.   *Ibid.*

nature and man, a separated nature and society then
rethought "by analogy" and by the image of a
primitive (naive-mischievous, rational-irrational)
who compels nature to produce by transforming it
through labor or manipulating it through signs.
Projected here is the worst Western psychology, our
own melange of rational pragmatism and supersti-
tious obsession. It is hard to imagine for what
"mysterious reason," as Godelier says, control of
forces could coexist with a rational operation, if not
by his own magic of "the interior and indivisible
unity" above. It is not true for archaic agriculture, as
Vernant demonstrates in *Travail et nature dans la
Gréce ancienne:* nor, *a fortiori*, for the primitive
hunter or farmer. Like the Greek peasant, the
primitive "contributes much less to the harvest by his
pains than by the periodic repetition of rites and
festivals."[25] Neither land nor effort is a "factor of
production." Effort is not "invested labor power"
recovered many times over in value at the end of a
production process. It is in a different form as full of
ritual as the exchange-gift *lost* and *given* without
economic calculation of return and compensation.
And the fruits of the harvest are not its "equivalent."
As by an excess, they maintain exchange (the
symbolic coherence of the group with the gods and
nature). Moreover, part of the harvest will immediately be returned as first-fruits in the process of
sacrifice and consumption in order to preserve this
symbolic movement. Above all, it must never be
interrupted because nothing is ever taken from
nature without being returned to it. Primitive man
does not chop one tree or trace one furrow without

---

25.   Vernant, *Travail et nature dans la Grèce ancienne*. [I
have been unable to complete this citation. Translator's note]

"appeasing the spirits" with a counter-gift or sacrifice. This taking and returning, giving and
receiving, is essential. It is always an actualization of
symbolic exchange through gods. The final product
is never aimed for. There is neither behavior aiming
to produce useful values for the group through
technical means, nor behavior aiming at the same
end by magical means. (This is really why there is no
scarcity. Scarcity only exists in our own *linear*
perspective of the accumulation of goods. Here it
suffices that the *cycle* of gifts and counter-gifts is not
interrupted.) And it is simply absurd to define
primitive activity as abstract subjectivity (utility) or
objective transformation (labor or suppletory
magic). Magic in the sense that we understand it, as
a direct objective appropriation of natural forces, is
a concept only negatively determined by our rational
concept of labor. To articulate magic and labor in
one "interior and indivisible unity" only seals their
disjunction. It ultimately disqualifies primitive
symbolic practices as irrational in opposition to
rational labor.

As in the case of objects, a simple observation of
historical decantation produces the materialist stage
of the "real" domination of nature. Marx says, "All
mythology masters and dominates and shapes the
forces of nature in and through imagination, hence
it disappears as soon as man gains mastery over the
forces of nature . . . : is Achilles possible side by side
with powder and lead? Or is the *Iliad* at all
compatible with the printing press and steam
press?"[26] This crushing argument masks the entire
problematic of the symbolic under a functionalist,

---

26. *Contribution to a Critique of Political Economy, op.cit.*,
pp. 310-311.

finalist retrospective view of mythology (and magic) in which it only awaits man's rational and technical domination in order to disappear.[27]

Epistemology III:

Materialism and Ethnocentrism

We must now pose again the problem of the general epistemology of historical materialism.

1. Marx outlined the formula for it, precisely in relation to labor, in the *Grundrisse:* "The conception of labor in this general form — as labor as such — is also immeasurably old. Nevertheless, when it is economically conceived in this simplicity, 'labor' is as modern a category as are the relations which create this simple abstraction... This example of labor shows strikingly how even the most abstract categories, despite their validity — precisely because of their abstractness — for all epochs, are nevertheless, in the specific character of this abstraction, themselves likewise a product of historical relations, and possess then full validity only for and within these relations."[28] What does it mean to say "valid for all epochs" but "fully applicable only for some"? This is the same mystery as the simultaneous subordination of infra- and superstructure, and the dialectical coexistence of a dominance and a determination in the last instance. If "the institution of the individual as laborer, in this nudity, is itself a historical product" (Marx), if "labor is not a real

---

27.   Besides the fact that mythology is here simply relegated to an illusory and provisional superstructure, it is completely untrue that the "real" domination of nature makes the "imaginary" disappear, for the good reason that it generates a fundamental contradiction connected with its abstractness and its very rationality, which primitive symbolic exchange, *which is more concrete in this respect*, does not have.

28.   *Grundrisse, op.cit.,* pp. 103-105.

category of tribal economy,"[29] then how could the concept of labor be applicable because of "its very abstractness"? This abstraction is precisely what creates the problem. At the same time that it produces the abstract universality of labor (of labor power), our epoch produces the universal abstraction of the *concept* of labor and the retrospective illusion of the validity of this concept for all societies. Concrete, actual, limited validity is that of an *analytic* concept; its abstract and unlimited validity is that of an *ideological* concept. This distinction concerns not only labor but the whole conceptual edifice of historical materialism: production, productive forces, mode of production, infrastructure (not to mention the dialectic and history itself). All these concepts are in fact historical products. Beyond the field that produced them (especially if they want to be "scientific"), they are only the metalanguage of a Western culture (Marxist, to be sure) that speaks from the height of its abstraction.

2. Nevertheless, it is not a matter of a simple exportation or extrapolation of concepts. Marx clarifies his approach in the same passage. "Bourgeois society is the most developed and the most complex historic organization of production. The categories which express its relation, the comprehension of its structure, thereby allows insights into the structure and relations of production of all the vanished social formations out of whose ruins and elements it built itself up, whose partly still unconquered remnants are carried along with it, whose mere nuances have developed explicit significance within it, etc. Human anatomy contains a key to the

---

29. M. Sahlins, *op.cit.*, p. 679.

anatomy of the ape. The intimations of higher
development among the subordinate species,
however, can be understood only after the higher
development is already known."[30]

Althusser saw in this passage a theoretical revolution in relation to navie genetic evolutionism. This
is certainly so, and evolutionism is dead. But isn't
this retroactive structuralism still an ideological
process, now in the sense of a *structural reconstruction through a simulation model* instead of
empiricist, finalist evolutionism? First, it is not
certain that the comparison with the anatomy of the
ape is anything more than a metaphor. What
guarantees the permanence of the same scheme of
intelligibility when one goes from the bio-anatomical
sphere to the human one of symbolism and historical
societies? Nothing is less certain: this is no more
certain than that the adult can comprehend the
child only in terms of the adult. In any case, in the
presupposition of this continuity there is a (positivist)
alignment of all analytic approaches with those of
the so-called exact sciences. If one does not admit
this hypothesis and maintains a specificity of
meaning and of the symbolic, Marxism contains a
miscomprehension of a rupture far more profound
than the one Althusser detects.

But let us return to the central argument. Does
the capitalist economy retrospectively illuminate
medieval, ancient, and primitive societies? No:
starting with the economic and production as the
determinant instance, other types of organization
are illuminated only in terms of this model and not
in their specificity or even, as we have seen in the
case of primitive societies, *in their irreducibility to*

---

30. *Grundrisse, op.cit.*, p. 105.

production. The magical, the religious, and the symbolic are relegated to the margins of the economy. And even when the symbolic formations expressly aim, as in primitive exchange, to prevent the emergence with the rise of economic structures of a transcendent social power that would escape the group's control, things are arranged nonetheless so as to see a determination by the economic in the last instance. Models never go beyond their shadows. Be it infinitely diversified and complicated, a model of political economy never permits us to go beyond political economy or to grasp what is on this side of it (or elsewhere).[31] Marx's phrase "bourgeois society, etc." is symptomatic. It assumes productivity in all societies, at least a kernel of it, from which the model of political economy can radiate. If this were true, political economy would be totally correct. If it is not true, this structural implantation of the mode of production can only make the specific reality of a given type of society burst into satellitized, disjointed categories (then rearticulated in terms of relative autonomy and dominance). Science will be vindicated, but at what price? The old finalism is not dead. It has simply moved from a finality of contents (traditional evolutionism) to a structural finality of the model and the analysis itself.

3. We have a new objection to deal with: it is not the model of political economy itself that permits the illumination of earlier societies; it is the *analysis of their contradictions* (which for Marx is the same

---

31. The impossibility for historical materialism of going beyond political economy toward the past as evidenced by its incapacity to decipher primitive societies, applies as well for the future by the same logic. It appears more and more incapable of outlining a revolutionary perspective truly beyond political economy. It flounders "dialectically" in the impasses of capital, just as it flounders in the miscomprehension of the symbolic.

thing as the analysis of their structures). (Let us say in passing that the metaphor of the ape is worthless — certainly the ape's anatomical structure cannot be illuminated starting from the "contradictions" of human anatomy.) In the same passage Marx says: "Although it is true, therefore, that the categories of bourgeois economics possess a truth for all other forms of society, this is to be taken only with a grain of salt. They can contain them in a developed, or stunted, or caricatured form etc., but always with an essential difference. The so-called historical presentation of development is founded, as a rule, on the fact that the latest form regards the previous ones as steps leading up to itself, and, since it is only rarely and only under quite specific conditions able to criticize itself...it always conceives them one-sidedly. The Christian religion was able to be of assistance in reaching an objective understanding of earlier mythologies only when its own self-criticism had been accomplished to a certain degree... Likewise, bourgeois economics arrived at an understanding of feudal, ancient, oriental economics only after the self-criticism of bourgeois society had begun."[32] Hence the crisis and the analysis of the crisis is what permits the comprehension of earlier societies in their difference and originality. Although this appears incontestable, it still participates in the critical and dialectical illusion.

Western culture was the first to critically reflect upon itself (beginning in the 18th century). But the effect of this crisis was that it reflected on itself also as a culture *in the universal*, and thus all other cultures were entered in its museum as vestiges of its

---

32.   *Grundrisse, op.cit.,* p. 106.

own image. It "estheticized" them, reinterpreted them on its own model, and thus precluded the radical interrogation these "different" cultures implied for it. The limits of this culture "critique" are clear: its reflection on itself leads only to the universalization of its own principles. Its own contradictions lead it, as in the previous case, to the world-wide economic and political imperialism of all modern capitalist and socialist Western societies. The limits of the materialist interpretation of earlier societies are the same. Those who have discovered primitive and savage arts have proved their good will and have shown all the lucidity one could ask about the art's originality and complexity. Without bias, they have attempted to "relocate" these "works" into their magical and religious "context." In the kindest yet most radical way the world has ever seen, they have placed these objects in a museum by implanting them in an esthetic category. But these objects are not art at all. And, precisely their non-esthetic character could at last have been the starting point for a *radical perspective* on (and not an *internal critical* perspective leading only to a broadened reproduction of) Western culture. Hence in the materialist interpretation there is only a replacement of "art" by "economics," "the esthetic virus" by "the virus of production and the mode of production." What has been said of the one applies equally to the other. The analysis of the contradictions of Western society has not led to the comprehension of earlier societies (or of the Third World). It has succeeded only in exporting these contradictions to them.[33] We agree with Marx when he says

---

33. At times not even the contradictions have been exported but very simply the *solution*, that is, the productivist model. But are not the contradictions part of the definition and functioning

that there is a correlation between the analysis of our
society's contradictions and the comprehension of
earlier societies, but only if we note the *partial* level
at which they both remain within historical
materialism. The blindness about primitive societies
is necessarily linked to a weakness in the radical
critique of political economy. This explains why,
having failed to subvert the foundations of political
economy, historical materialism results only in
reactivating its model at a world-wide level (even if
this model is dialectical and charged with
contradictions). Through its most "scientific"[34]

---

of the productivist model?

34.   The most advanced bourgeois thought also exports its
models (its viruses) under the cover of the most "objective"
critical epistemology. "For if the final aim of anthropology is to
contribute to a better knowledge of objectified thought and its
mechanisms, it is in the last resort immaterial whether in this
book the thought processes of the South American Indians take
place through the medium of theirs. What matters is that the
human mind, regardless of the identity of those who happen to
be giving it expression, should display an increasingly intelligible
structure as a result of the double reflexive forward movement of
two thought processes acting one upon the other, either of which
can in turn provide the spark or tinder whose conjunction will
shed light on both. And should this light happen to reveal a
treasure, there will be no need of an arbitrator to parcel it out,
since, as I declared at the outset, the heritage is untransferable
and cannot be split up" (Lévi-Strauss, *The Raw and the Cooked*,
trans. J. and D. Weightman [New York: Harper and Row,
1969], pp. 13-14). This is the extreme of liberal thought and the
most beautiful way of preserving the initiative and priority of
Western thought within "dialogue" and under the sign of the
universality of the human mind (as always for Enlightenment
anthropology). Here is the beautiful soul! Is it possible to be more
impartial in the sensitive and intellectual knowledge of the
other? This harmonious vision of two thought processes renders
their *confrontation* perfectly inoffensive, by denying the
difference of the primitives as an element of rupture with and
subversion of (our) "objectified thought and its mechanisms."

inclinations toward earlier societies, it "naturalizes" them under the sign of the mode of production. Here again their anthropological relegation to a museum, a process originated in bourgeois society, continues under the sign of its critique.

IV. ON THE ARCHAIC AND FEUDAL MODE

The Slave

The status of the slave is analyzed by Marxist theory retrospectively, starting from the status of the salaried worker. The latter does not dispose of his labor, nor of the product of his labor; but he does dispose of his labor power, which he can alienate (although not his person which is his property). For his part, the slave disposes neither of the one nor the other. Thus he is being defined as a function of the distinction between labor and labor power (*which will be developed later*), as the sum of these two elements alienated to the master. And the specificity of slavery resides, by deduction, in the master's ownership of the slave's labor power. But this is only an analytic reconstruction. Because one reunites two elements consequently separated, it does not follow that their sum clarifies the earlier state. The radical difference is precisely that *they were not separated* and that what comes to pass from the separation is not readable through anticipation, except by an abuse of analytical power. We are faced again with a presumption of the economic through the grid labor-labor power. The symbolic relation master-slave is conceived as a kind of husk whose "real" kernel will be extracted in the thread of history (in fact, in the thread of the theoretical model that will impose this principle of reality). What is lost in this process is everything that is exchanged in the master-slave relation and everything not reducible to the alienation-exploitation of a labor power.

The fact that the slave is not separated from the master in the manner of the free laborer implies that the master is not separated from the slave in the manner of the free proprietor (or employer). Neither the one nor the other has the respective status of the individual and individual liberty neither confronts one another as such—which is the definition of alienation. A relation of reciprocity exists between them—not in the modern and psychological sense of a bi-univocal relation of two individualized subjects, that is, in the individualism-altruism context that circumscribes our morality—but in the sense of an *obligation*, of a structure of exchange and obligation where the specification of the terms of exchange in autonomous subjects, where the partition (as we know it), does not yet exist. This is the level of the symbolic and not of autonomous subjects of exchange, nor of an object of exchange (labor power, nourishment, protection) autonomizable as a commodity.[1] Instead, there is a dual structure in which neither the abstraction of value nor the imaginary identity of subjects comes into play.

The free worker finds his identity in the mirror of his labor power. His property, his "liberation" as a worker, signifies his accession to privatized

---

1. The same problem applies to the domestic "labor" of women in patriarchal society. There is neither juridical individuality nor a contract; nor possible autonomization of labor and its product *as a value* beyond the personal relation and the reciprocal obligation. The desire to assimilate these prestations with the exercise or the exploitation of labor power amounts to a political abstraction.

individuality, that is, to alienation. He is alienated not insofar as he sells his labor power, but insofar as he is an owner, "disposing" of it as if it were his own goods. For finally what is it that allows me to dispose of myself if not "privation" (the right of the privatized individual who is isolated from others)? This is an exorbitant privilege, which the master never had over the slave, since it is only with slave-trading, that is, when slavery is included within a market economy, that the master "disposes" of the slave to the point of being able to alienate him like other commodities. When one analyzes this stage, it is already a market economy that one is analyzing and not the stage that is specific to slavery. In the original relation, the slave, or rather the relation master-slave, is *unalienable* in the sense that neither the master nor the slave are alienated from each other, nor is the slave alienated from himself as is the free worker in the private disposition of his labor power.

In every sense, "liberation" is thus characterized as the process of the interiorization of the separation, of the interiorization of a subjective, abstract essence (in this case, labor power) over which the identity of the subject comes to fix itself. The stave's status is not of this kind. He is *connected* and the sovereignty of the master is not the transcendence of authority as we know it; it is a personal domination that must not be confused with the scheme of master subject and of slave object (which is our form of rational and contractual exchange in which each subject is an object for the other). Domination, as distinct from alienation and exploitation, does not involve the objectification of the dominated, but an obligation that always carries an element of reciprocity.

We have a tendency to reinterpret the relation of
slavery (or servitude) as the maximum limit of
exploitation and alienation in comparison to our
economic configuration and our psychology of
subject and object. We consider the passage to
salaried labor as "liberation" and objective,
historical progress. Yet this view participates in the
illusion of Western humanist rationality, a
rationality incarnated in the thread of history by the
abstract, political State which, when instituted,
attributes all earlier forms of domination to the
irrational. But it is not true that domination is only
an archaic and barbaric form of power. The concept
of power with all that it implies about the
abstraction and alienation of social relations, about
exploiter-exploited relations, etc., has value, strictly
speaking, only when applied to our kind of social
organization. To project it indiscriminately on
earlier forms of domination, explaining the
differences as some historical underdevelopment, is
to miscomprehend all that the earlier formations can
teach us about the symbolic operation of social
relations.

The Artisan

The status of the artisan is defined not only by the
ownership of his "labor power" (as distinct from the
slave) but, as distinct from the salaried worker, by
the ownership of his "instruments of production."
He controls his "means of production" and the process of his "labor." Only the distribution and
commercialization of the product escape him — not
wholly however, since if the process of production
develops in the framework of an integrated
community (the corporation), the processes of
distribution and consumption always take place in

the cadre of integrated personal relations (self-sub-sistence, family, tribe, village, neighborhood). This determination is at least as important as the strict "juridical ownership of the means of production" in defining the artisanal mode.[2] At the stage of artisan exchange, there is still a collective mode to personal relations in which the circulation of products, though mediated by money, still does not have the general equivalence of commodities, just as the people who make the exchanges still do not have the status of equivalence with respect to a market. That is the basic definition of the artisan class: a mode of social relations in which not only is the process of production controlled by the producer but in which the *collective process remains internal to the group*, and in which producers and consumers are the same people, above all defined through the reciprocity of the group. This situation can be illustrated by the example of language. Language is not produced by certain people and consumed by others; everyone is at the same time a producer and a consumer. In fact, there are neither producers nor consumers and what is established is not the general equivalence of individuals *vis-à-vis* language, but an immediate reciprocity of exchange *through language*.[3]

---

2. In a certain way, the moment of consumption remains of the artisan type even in the system of our political economy. The user who consumes enters into personal relationship with the product and directly recovers its "use value," just as the process of artisan labor preserves the use value of the labor power of the artisan. But this personal exchange in consumption is restricted for us to the level of the privatized individual. This also remains the only moment that seems to avoid exchange value, hence it is invested today with a very strong psychological and social charge.

3. Language is thus not a "means" of communication (no more than the tool is a "means" of production for the artisan or

In the primitive exchange gift, the status of goods that circulate is close to language. The goods are neither produced nor consumed as values. Their function is the continuous articulation of the exchange. The situation is not completely the same in artisanal exchange since goods there already have a finality of use and a value. But something remains of the personal quality of the exchange that does not permit distinguishing production and consumption as two separated functions. Just as one cannot speak of the relation of the blacksmith to his hammer, or of the relation of the peasant to the plow or his land, as a relation to "means of production," so the relation of the artisan to his work is not one "productive force" applied to the other "forces of production." It is clear moreover that neither the product, nor the instrument, nor the operation itself can be dissociated from the personal relationship in which they occur. All the categories above only serve to rationalize the situation.

It is even false to say that in artisanal work the artisan is "master of his labor" and "product of his labor." For he is not in the situation of an autonomous individual, in a position of "control," that is, of productive exteriority. To define "work" as a process of concrete labor, in opposition to industrial labor, is not enough. It is *something other than labor*. Just as there is no separation between the sphere of producers and the sphere of consumers, so there is no true separation between labor power and the product, between the position of the subject and of the object. The artisan lives his work as a relation

_____

the primitive). Nor are individuals thinkable as separated terms outside the exchange of language. At this level, language is a symbolic form and it is so not, as is generally thought, in its coded signification function, nor in its structural agency.

of symbolic exchange, abolishing the definition of himself as "laborer" and the object as "product of his labor." Something in the material that he works is a continuous response to that which he does, escaping all productive finality (which purely and simply transforms materials into use value or exchange value). There is something that eludes the law of value and bears witness to a kind of reciprocal prodigality. In his work, what he bestows is lost and given and rendered, expended and resolved and abolished, but not "invested."

All of this is clarified further through the problem of the work of art about which historical materialism, fixated in the scheme of production, has only been able to comment with respect to its mode of socio-historical determination, mechanistic or structural, never being able to account for the moment of its operation and of its radical difference. But this is also true, to a lesser extent, of artisanal work (according to etymology, "demiurge"), which draws a radical difference between work and labor. *Work is a process of destruction as well as of "production,"* and in this way work is symbolic. Death, loss and absence are inscribed in it through this dispossession of the subject, this loss of the subject and the object in the scansion of the exchange. Starting from the concepts of production and labor, we will never grasp what happens there in the negation of labor, the negation of the law of value, in the destruction of value. The work of art and to a certain extent the artisanal work bear in them the inscription of the loss of the finality of the subject and the object, the radical compatibility of life and death, the play of an ambivalence that the product of labor as such does not bear since it has inscribed in it only the finality of value.

The world of production, our world, has eliminated this ambivalence. To project it everywhere else is a theoretically fraudulent operation, but also a failure to the extent that it annihilates its object in order to avoid its radical contradiction. All materialist writing bears the stigmas of the rigidity and the silence that it imposes on its object.

In relation to the Greek city, J.-P. Vernant suggests a very important series of elements pertaining to the status of the demiurge and labor.

The unity of the polis is not based on a distribution of tasks, a division of labor, a functional differentiation, but on a "philia," a political community of citizens defined as peers. There is no human or social function of labor. "The social bond is established beyond the craft at that level where the citizens can reciprocally love one another."[4] The term "division of labor" itself is anachronistic here. It assumes a representation of the craft in relation to production in general, a functional differentiation into abstract, rational elements which is not the case. There is a distribution of tasks as a function of needs and capacities; each "labor" maintains its particular destination and does not have its meaning in reference to other "labor," but uniquely in its end, in the need of the user. The activity of labor is seen exclusively as a function of the use value of the manufactured product. It places the producer and the user in a more or less direct relationship. A personal bond of dependence, a relation of service, seems to be established between them. "From the perspective of use value, the product is not viewed as a function of the human labor that created it, as

4. Vernant, "Lé travail et la pensée technique," in *Mythe et pensée chez les Grecs, op.cit.*

crystallized labor. On the contrary, it is labor that is seen as a function of the product, as appropriate for the satisfaction of a given need of the user."[5] Demiurgical labor does not produce "value." It is a response to a demand (the need of the user) and is exhausted in this response. Articulated by the demand of the other, and articulating this demand, the object does not take on the status of value (sum of accumulated labor) that could circulate beyond this relation and enter as such into other equivalences. By way of summary, the problem is one of the best use of things, not of their transformation through labor. (Praxis, a noble activity, is always one of use, as distinct from poesis which designates fabrication. Only the former, which plays and acts, but does not produce, is noble.) The result is that in no way does "productivity" emerge. The division of tasks is never considered as a means of organizing production in order to obtain a maximum productivity from a given quantity of labor. Similarly, there is no "technical" autonomization of the instruments of labor. They do not have a technical status like our means of production, their *techne* is connected. They have neither technical thought, nor thought oriented toward indefinite progress.

All these facts converge toward one point: the inadequacy of the concepts of labor, production, productive force, and relations of production in accounting for, let us say, pre-industrial organization (the same holds also for feudal or traditional organization). However, an objection can be made against Vernant. Breaking with the primacy of pro-

5.   *Ibid*. [I have not been able to locate the page reference. Translator's note]

duction and denouncing the tendency to impose it in
a context where it does not apply, Vernant transfers
the emphasis to needs and the finality of personal
use. It is these elements that define wealth and it is in
them that the personal relation (on which social
relations are based) is centered (and not in production, which is not significant). In the polis, two
persons are united under the sign of use value, rather
than in our economy, where the relation is put under
the sign of exchange value. In effect, this defines, for
us, the service relation.[6] But it is necessary to see
that the notion of service is still strongly impregnated
by our categories: economic categories since it
simply effects a transfer of exchange value to use
value; psychological categories since it preserves the
separation of the producer and the user, putting
them simply in an intersubjective relation.
"Personal" exchange is, in this case, only a psychological dimension that comes to connote or to
overdetermine properly economic exchange. (We see
this today with the "personalization" of exchanges,
the psychological designation of a relation as that of
two equivalent economic subjects.) And "service" is
only a moralized, altruistic scheme that preserves the
respective position of the subjects while seeking to go
beyond it.

Symbolic reciprocity is very different from this.
*The symbolic must never be confused with the
psychological.* The symbolic sets up a relation of
exchange in which the respective positions cannot be
autonomized:

---

6. Moreover, it is this notion of service that is everywhere
used as an excuse to revive the present system of exchange value,
that is, the fiction (it can only be a fiction for us) of a personal
exchange mediated only by use value.

- neither the producer and his product;
- nor the producer and the user;
- nor the producer and his "concrete" essence, his labor power;
- nor the user and his "concrete" essence, his needs;
- nor the product and its "concrete" finality, its utility.

All these distinctions, which are evident in psychology and political economy, are excluded by symbolic relations.

Abstract social labor creating exchange value by the mediation of the whole system of capital is the formula of our political economy. Labor-use value creating product-use value in a direct relation of producer and user is the formula of the artisan mode according to Vernant. This is still an economic formula. In our contemporary ideology of service it functions in the first instance purely and simply as a bonus and excuse, just as use value in general serves as an excuse for exchange value. Symbolic relations call both formulas into question. To the extent that Vernant restricts the originality of the artisan form as in the second formula, he allows himself to avoid its specifically symbolic character, its irreducibly non-economic nature.

The materialist rewriting of the slave or the artisan (of the slave or feudal-artisanal mode) has serious consequences to the extent that schemas of "liberation" and transcendence, which are in reality repressive schemas, develop from it. We have seen how the reinterpretation of slavery in terms of the expropriation of labor power led to considering its reappropriation by the "free" laborer as absolute progress in the human order. This relegates servi-

tude to an absolute barbarism, fortunately overcome
thanks to the development of productive forces. This
ideology of freedom remains the weak point of our
Western rationality, including Marxism.

Similarly, the conception of the artisan as "master
of his labor and of his production," as "subject of the
system of labor"[7] immediately implies the utopia of
a Golden Age of productive labor. But, there is no
"labor;" there is only the division of labor and the
sale of labor power. The truth of labor is its
capitalist definition. Starting from this definition,
the illusion is established of labor that *would be
nothing but labor*, one that can be reappropriated in
the totality of its process, as an artisanal alternative
to the capitalist system. In fact, this alternative
remains imaginary. It makes no reference at all to
what is symbolic in the mode of the artisan, but to
the artisan revised and corrected in terms of the
mastery and autonomy of the producer. But such
mastery is absurd since its definition encloses itself in
terms of labor and use value. The individual who
"controls" his labor is an idealization of this basic
constraint. It is simply the slave who has become *his
own master*, since the master-slave couple is interiorized in the same individual without ceasing to
function as an alienated structure. He "disposes" of
himself; he is his own usufruct. This is self-
management at the level of the individual producer,
but self-management as we know is nothing but the
metamorphosis of productive management. In its
collective form, it outlines today the Golden Age of
social-productivism. The self-management of the
artisan is only the Golden Age of the small,

individual producer, the apotheosis of the "instinct of workmanship."

But this nostalgic view of the artisan is not the deed of a few esthetes or intellectuals. All worker demands that transcend wage demands even a little aim, in this sense, at a reappropriation of the labor process, if not of the product. Through working conditions, "job enrichment," the questioning of assembly-line work, the control of work rates and investments, etc., it is always a matter of becoming again "the subject of the labor system." Proudhon had envisaged "the polyvalence by which the worker, accomplishing the whole cycle of production, would become once again the master of the complete process." Whether this demand today is individual (it gets stranded in the potter or the neo-artisan), communal or collective, it is always the ideal of a reappropriation of labor and this ideal depends on sublimation. It perpetuates, under the autonomy of the laborer, the principle of the sublimation of labor. It is contemporaneous, in the shadow of the industrial system and its constraints, with the manipulated resurrection of the body and sexuality in which each becomes again the master of his body and the free agent of his pleasure, at once interiorizing the sexual *function* and reinvesting the body as the *instrument of the production* of pleasure. Once again there is outlined a Golden Age of functional and productive Eros. In both cases, we have repressive desublimation.[8]

---

8. The phantasm of leisure as an autonomous activity and the phantasm of a purely technical division of labor as a social ideal of transparency obviously depend on the same schema. One can even ask oneself if the perspective that Marx outlines of a realm beyond the division of labor is nothing but a *polyvalent* extension of the autonomous status of the individual artisan:

Does the freedom to "function" sexually constitute a revolution? Does the mastery of the process of production constitute a revolution? One thing is certain: autonomous or not, master of himself or not (individually or collectively), labor can only inscribe in production a sublimated Eros, or in the case of the phantasm of self-management, a repressively desublimated Eros.

Epistemology IV:

Marxism and Miscomprehension

"The idea that in all societies the relations of production, and consequently, politics, law, religion, etc., presuppose that in all societies the same articulation of human activities exists, that technology, law, politics, and religion are always necessarily separated and separable; it is to extrapolate to the totality of history the structuration of our own society, which is inevitably meaningless outside of it." This summarizes the critique that we have made, in the sense that it aims less at the contents of the analysis than at the form, less at any particular conclusion than at the "scientific" tendency itself.[9] The dialectical structuring of

---

". . .in communist society. . .society regulates the general production and thus makes it possible for me to do one thing today and another tomorrow, to hunt in the morning, fish in the afternoon, rear cattle in the evening, criticize after dinner, just as I have a mind, without ever becoming hunter, fisherman, shepherd, or critic" (*The German Ideology, op.cit.,* p. 22). It is an ideal of freedom and of disposability, an ideal of the achievement of a subject, a humanist project that would not contradict bourgeois, liberal thought in its better moments. And who will rule "the general production?"

9.   Cardan, pseudonym for Cornélius Castoriadis, editor of *Socialisme ou Barbarie,* 1949-1965. [Translator's note]

categories which remain in a latent state, with its latent hierarchy placing the determinant instance at the heart of the process of development, as separated functions, as distinctive oppositions ruled by the code, whether traditional or Marxist, carries an incurable *ethnocentrism of the code*. It is at this price that "materialist" analysis aspires to be a science, to be intelligible; but this intelligibility is that of its own code. From the outset it labors in fact to reproduce it, while at the same time compressing its object, scotomizing it, arming itself against it with a whole system of defenses and miscomprehensions. It works *in the imaginary* like the man who, having lost his key in a dark alley, looks for it in a lighted area because, he says, that it is the only place where he could find it. Thus, historical materialism does not know how to grasp earlier societies in their symbolic articulation. It only finds in them what it could find under its own light, that is, its artificial mode of production.

This miscomprehension is not a peripheral or secondary weakness. (The deepest racist avatar is to think that an error about earlier societies is politically or theoretically less serious than a misinterpretation of our own world. Just as a people that oppresses another cannot be free, so a culture that is mistaken about another must also be mistaken about itself. This is only another way of formulating Marx's equation between the level of the analysis of contradictions and the comprehension of the specificity of other societies.) In effect, the miscomprehension, moving from societies "without history" to archaic or feudal formations, nurtures a *theoretical, political and strategic miscomprehension of capitalist formations themselves*. It is a shortcoming of historical materialism in accounting for the strategic configuration of modern societies which echoes in its incapacity to account for the symbolic organization of earlier formations. And it does not help to say that "it has other fish to fry." That is, historical materialism has the critique of the capitalist economy and its relations of production as its object and primitive societies, kinship, language and the symbolic, are not its province. Historical materialism must be held responsible, *by its own standards*, for the carelessness and error that it perpetuates in all these domains for through these miscomprehensions, to which it is an accomplice, its own object then eludes it. It is the contradictions of this object, repressed and mystified, that become the basis for analyzing historical materialism rather than that which analyzes them. It therefore is not a matter of accidental or venal shortcomings: the repression of the symbolic nourishes all the rationalist political illusions, all the *dreams of political voluntarism*, that are born in the terrain of historical materialism.

Along with Cardan one can offer the still more radical hypothesis that not only have the categories of historical materialism no meaning outside of our society, but that *perhaps in a fundamental way they no longer have any meaning for us*. To the extent that they function at the interior of our reality principle, which is the principle of separation (this is where its analytic — indeed, "scientific" — efficacy resides), they blind us along the line of separation itself, along this fracture of the symbolic, along this place (or non-place: utopia) beneath (or beyond) the economy and the internal contradictions of the mode of production. Materialist logic, seeing only the contradictions that are accessible to dialectical or structural schemas, perhaps sees only the *symptoms*, at the interior of the system, of that rupture which founds the system itself. The political significance of this critique is that the struggle at the level of these contradictions-symptoms does not touch their basis, which is separation. This struggle is only an accomodation that launches the well-known cycle of the extended reproduction of the contradictions and the system itself. The "dialectical" revolution in the order of the mode of production is only perhaps the symptomatic discourse of the separation. Historical materialism prohibits itself from seeing this. It is incapable of thinking the process of ideology, of culture, of language, of the symbolic in general. It misses the point not only with regard to primitive societies, but it also fails to account for the radicality of the separation in our societies, and therefore the radicality of the subversion that grows there.

V. MARXISM AND THE SYSTEM OF POLITICAL ECONOMY

A Euclidean Geometry of History?

Historical materialism emerges in a society ruled by the capitalist mode, a stage of actualization knotted by contradictions connected to the mode of production and to the final catastrophe of the class struggle. It wishes to decipher the ultimate phase of political economy and aims at its abolition. A theoretical reason and a universal practice, a dialectic of productive forces and relations of production, a continuous logic of contradiction, a homogenous space of positivity and negativity—all of this (and the concept of history itself) is organized according to the idea that, with the mode of capitalist production, the universal process approaches its truth and its end. Earlier modes of production are never envisaged as autonomous or definitive; it is unthinkable that history could have been arrested with them. The dialectic limits them to being no more than successive phases in a process of revolution that is also a cumulative process of production. The capitalist mode does not escape this inexorable logic, but it assumes, nonetheless, an absolute privilege to the extent that the other modes of production have only cleared the way for the fundamental contradiction between the production of social wealth and the production of social relations, and for the possibility for men finally to resolve their social existence *in its real terms*. In earlier formations, men blindly produced their social relations at the same time as their material wealth. The capitalist mode is the moment when they become conscious of this double and simultaneous production, when they aim to take it under rational control. No earlier society had posed this question in these terms; hence, none could resolve it. They could not have knowledge of the end of history because they lived neither historically nor within the mode of production. This is why they were really only precursors; their truth was already beyond them in the future concept of history, and in its content, the determination of the social relation by material production. This concept would appear only in the final stages of capitalism and in its critique, illuminating in one stroke the entire earlier process. Capital is thus an end and all history is gathered in the final process of its abolition. Or better, it is the only mode of production whose critique becomes possible in its real terms; this is why the revolution that puts an end to it is definitive.

Behind all of this there lie two postulates:

— A process of historical development is already there in all earlier societies (a mode of production, contradictions, a dialectic) but they do not produce a concept of it and hence do not transcend it.

— The moment of becoming conscious of the process (the production of the critical concept connected to the conditions of the capitalist formation) is also the decisive stage of its revolution.

All of this is perfectly Hegelian and one can raise questions about the type of necessity that makes the fundamental contradiction connected to the determinant instance of the economy, which is already "objectively" at work in earlier societies, become manifest at the same time as the discourse capable of founding it theoretically (historical materialism). As if by chance, the *reality* of the mode of production enters the scene at the moment when someone is discovered who invents the *theory* of it. As if by chance, at the same moment that the class struggle enters its overt and decisive phase, it discovers the theory that takes account of it scientifically and objectively (whereas the blind and latent class struggles in earlier societies only produced ideologies). This conjunction is a little too neat and irresistibly evokes the Hegelian trajectory in which the saga of Spirit is completely illuminated retrospectively, only to culminate in the discourse of Hegel himself.

This conjunction of analysis and "objective reality" ("Communism is the movement of the real itself.") is only the materialist variant of our culture's pretention to the privilege of being closer than any other culture to the universal, closer to the end of history or truth. This rationalist eschatology, which takes its bearings on the irreversibility of a linear temporality of accumulation and unveiling is *par excellence* that of science. The phantasm of science is double: on the one hand, there is an "epistemological break" that relegates all other thought to a senseless prehistory of knowledge and, simultaneously, on the other hand, there is a linear accumulation of knowledge, hence of truth as a final totalization. This procedure allows our society to think itself and live itself as superior to all others. It is not only *relatively* more advanced by the fact that our society succeeds them, but *absolutely* more advanced because, as the holder of the *theory* of this objective finality of science or history, it reflects itself *in the universal*, taking itself as end and, hence retrospectively, as the principle of explication of earlier formations.

The materialist theory of history cannot escape from ideology. We have arrived at the moment of objectivity, the truth of history, the revolutionary denouement. But what authorizes science in its scorn of magic or alchemy, for example, in this disjunction of a truth to come, of a destiny of objective knowledge, hidden from the infantile miscomprehension of earlier societies? And what authorizes the "science of history" to claim this disjunction of a history to come, of an objective finality that robs earlier societies of the determinations in which they live, of their magic, of their difference, of the meaning that they attribute to themselves, in order to clarify them in the infrastructural truth of the mode of production to which we alone have the key? The culmination produced by Marxist analysis, in which it illuminates the demise of all contradictions, is *simply the emergence of history*, that is, a process in which everything is always said to be resolved at a later date by an accumulated truth, a determinant instance, an irreversible history. Thus, history can only be, at bottom, the equivalent of the ideal point of reference that, in the classical and rational perspective of the Renaissance, allows the spatial imposition of an arbitrary, unitary structure. And historical materialism could only be the Euclidean geometry of this history.

It is only in the *mirror* of production and history, under the double principle of indefinite accumulation (production) and dialectical continuity (history), only by the arbitrariness of the *code*, that our Western culture can reflect itself in the universal as the privileged moment of truth (science) or of revolution (historical materialism). Without this simulation, without this gigantic reflexivity of the concave (or convex) concept of history or production, our era loses all privileges. It would not be any closer to any term of knowledge or any social truth than any other.

Here, it is not a question of an ideal vantage point on historical materialism. Rather it is a matter of knowing if historical materialism (history made dialectical by the mode of production) does not itself constitute an ideal vantage point, that is, the point of view of a reductive ideality of all social formations, including our own. This is why it is important to begin with this *ethnological reduction* and to strip our culture, including its materialist critique, of the absolute privilege that it gives itself by the imposition of a universal code (the strategic element of this code being the conjunction, under the sign of truth, of theory and reality, or of "critical" theory and "real" contradictions).

Returning to Marx, Althusser develops this theory of a moment of history (our own) when science exists in an immediate form of consciousness, when truth can be read in an open book of phenomena. In opposition to all prevous modes, says Althusser, the capitalist mode constitutes "the exceptional, specific present in which *scientific abstractions exist in the state of empirical realities.* The historical epoch of the foundation of the science of Political Economy does seem here to be brought into relationship with experience itself (*Erfahrung*), i.e., with the straight-forward reading of the essence in the phenomenon. Or, if you prefer, the sectional reading of the relationship with the essence of a particular epoch of human history in which the generalization of commodity production and hence of the category commodity appears simultaneously as the absolute

condition of possibility and the immediate given of
this direct reading from experience."[1] In the
citation on the anatomy of the ape and in the
analysis of Aristotle's concept of value, Marx
evidences this position: "It requires a fully developed
production of commodities before, *from experience*
alone, the *scientific truth* springs up. . ."[2] If it is in
the epistemological break that Marxist discourse is
founded as science, this break is only possible "in a
society in which the commodity form has become the
general form of the produce of labor."[3] Hence
(Althusser): "If the present form of capitalist
production has produced scientific truth itself in its
invisible reality (*Wirklichkeit, Erscheinung, Erfahrung*), in its self-consciousness, its own phenomenon is therefore its own self-criticism in act (*en
acte*)—then it is perfectly clear why the present's
retrospection of the past is no longer ideology but
true knowledge, and we can appreciate the *legiti-
mate epistemological primacy of the present over the
past.*"[4]

To this Marxist scientific position, one can object
in two ways:

1. One can admit that the epistemological break
which, made possible by a certain historical process
and in its own turn making possible the scientific
analysis of this process, marks not a "critical"
rupture but a vicious circularity. Through the
generalized commodity form, historical materialism
clarifies all the significations of our society as regu-
lated by the generalized commodity form (either by

1. *Reading Capital*, trans. B. Brewster (London: New Left
Books, 1972), p. 124.
2. *Ibid.*
3. *Ibid.*
4. *Ibid.*, p. 125.

the mode of production, or by the dialectic of history. It does not matter by which concept this circularity is known. In all cases, "science," beginning with its break, only describes the coincidence of the state of affairs that produced it and the scientific model that it outlines.). Is this the dialectic? Not at all. It is the self-verification of a model that is achieved through the adequacy of the rational (itself) and the real. In fact, this break of which Marxism avails itself is equivalent, as in all "science," to the establishment of a principle of rationality that is only the rationalization of its own process.

2. Instead of contesting historical materialism on its own explanation of itself (the pretension of being a scientific discourse founded on a certain historical development), one can agree with it. But with the addition that, strictly speaking, in Marx's time, the commodity form had not at all attained its generalized form, and has had a long history *since Marx*. Thus Marx was not in a historical position to speak scientifically, to speak the truth. In that case, another break imposes itself, one that would risk making Marxism appear as a theory of a surpassed stage of commodity production, hence, as an ideology. At least, if one wanted to be scientific!

In the first case one challenges completely the validity of Marxist concepts (history, dialectic, mode of production, etc.) as an arbitrary model that verifies itself, like any self-respecting model, by its own circularity. One challenges historical materialism in its form and it falls to the level of an ideology. In the second case, one preserves the fundamental *form* of the Marxist critique of political economy but forces its *content* to break out beyond that of material production alone. In this hypothesis one

can admit that, since Marx, there has been just such
an extension of the sphere of productive forces, or
better, of the sphere of political economy (in which
consumption as the production of signs, needs,
knowledge, sexuality, is directly integrated, or on
the way toward integration, as productive forces). In
brief, so many things have erupted in the "infrastructure" that the distinction infra-superstructure
breaks down and today contradictions emerge at all
levels. Something in the capitalist sphere has
changed radically, something Marxist analysis can
no longer respond to. Hence, in order to survive it
must be revolutionized, something which certainly
has not been done since Marx.

This hypothesis is distinguished from the first by
maintaining that everything can still be explained by
a critique of political economy (but one that is
generalized) and in the perspective of historical
materialism (the instance of production). But,
extended to all domains and extracted radically
from its economistic tendency. This hypothesis,
which pushes Marx to the limit, may still not be
tenable. It is possible that the extension of the sphere
of productive forces, which amounts to a
radicalization of the concept, is such that the
concept itself would have to go. What would become
of the key concepts of historical materialism — infra-
superstructure, ideology, dialectic of the relations of
production, surplus value, class and class struggle —
when confronted by this generalized political
economy? Do they maintain such a coherence among
themselves and *with the historical era in which they
were born* that they become useless, even mystifying
for us? Perhaps political economy is inseparable
from the theory of the determinant instance of
material production, in which case the Marxist

critique of political economy is not extendable to a generalized theory.

The Third Phase of Political Economy

In *The Poverty of Philosophy*, Marx drew up a kind of genealogy of the system of exchange value:

1. Only the surplus of material production is exchanged (in archaic and feudal production, for example). Vast sectors remain outside the sphere of exchange and commodities.

2. The entire volume of "industrial" material production is alienated in the exchange (capitalist political economy).

3. Even what is considered unalienable (divided, but not exchanged) — virtue, love, knowledge, consciousness — also falls into the sphere of exchange value. This is the era of "general corruption," of "universal venality," "the time when each object, physical or moral, is brought to market as a commodity value in order to be priced at its exact value."

The schema is clear, beyond what Marx partially foresaw. Between phase 1 and phase 2 there is the birth of capital, a decisive change not only regarding the *extension* of the sphere of exchange, but also its repercussions at the level of social relations. Between phase 2 and phase 3, by contrast, Marx and Marxism see only a kind of extensive effect. The "infrastructural" mutation which sets the present mode of production and social relations into place, is achieved in phase 2 — phase 3 represents only the "superstructural" effect in the domain of "non-material" values. With Marx, and against him in some ways, we think that it is necessary to give this genealogy all of its analytical force.

There is a decisive mutation between phase 2 and phase 3. Phase 3 is as revolutionary in relation to phase 2 as phase 2 is in relation to phase 1. To the third power of the system of political economy corresponds a new type of social relations, a type that is different from the contradictions of phase 2, which is properly that of capital (and of *Capital*). In Marx's projection this new phase of political economy, which in his time had not yet fully developed, is immediately neutralized, drawn into the wake of phase 2, in terms of the market and "mercantile venality." Even today the only "Marxist" critique of culture, of consumption, of information, of ideology, of sexuality, etc. is made in terms of "capitalist prostitution," that is, in terms of commodities, exploitation, profit, money and surplus value. That is, terms characteristic of phase 2 and though reaching their full value there they only serve as a *metaphorical reference* when transferred as a principle of analysis to phase 3. Even the Situationists, without doubt the only ones to attempt to extract this new radicality of political economy in their "society of the spectacle," still refer to the "infrastructural" logic of the commodity. From this derives their fidelity to the proletariat, which is logical if, behind the organization of the spectacle, the exploitation of labor power is still determinant — the spectacle being only an immense connotation of the commodity. But this is illogical if the concept of the spectacle is taken *as that of the commodity*, as Marx did in his time, in all its radicality as a generalized process of social abstraction in which "material" exploitation is only one particular phase. In this hypothesis, it is the form-spectacle that is determinant since one begins with *the most developed structural phase*.[5] This step truly overturns perspectives regarding politics, revolution, the proletariat and social classes. But this is to accept or to allow at any rate that a revolution has occurred in the capitalist world without our Marxists having wanted to comprehend it. The objection that our society is still largely dominated by the logic of commodities is irrelevant. When Marx set out to analyze capital, capitalist industrial production was still largely a minority phenomenon. When he designated political economy as the determining sphere, religion was still largely dominant. The theoretical decision is never made at the quantitative level, but at the level of a structural critique.

This mutation concerns the passage from the form-commodity to the form-sign, from the abstraction of the exchange of material products under the law of general equivalence to the operationalization of all exchanges under the law of the code. With this passage to *the political economy of the sign*, it is not a matter of a simple "commercial prostitution" of all values (which is the completely romantic vision from the celebrated passage of the *Communist Manifesto*: capitalism tramples on all human values — art, culture, labor, etc. — in order to make money; the *romantic critique* of profit). It is a matter of the passage of all values to exchange-sign value, under the hegemony of the code. That is, of a structure of control and of power much more subtle and more totalitarian than that of exploitation. *For the sign is much more than a connotation of the commodity*, than a semiological supplement to

---

5. With his concept of "reification," Lukács, without doubt, constituted the only critical line of theoretical development among Marx and the Situationists.

exchange value. It is an operational structure that lends itself to a structural manipulation compared with which the quantitative mystery of surplus value appears inoffensive. The super-ideology of the sign and the general operationalization of the signifier — everywhere sanctioned today by the new master disciplines of structural linguistics, semiology, information theory, and cybernetics — has replaced good old political economy as the theoretical basis of the system. This new ideological structure, that plays on the hieroglyphs of the code, is much more illegible than that which played on productive energy. This manipulation, that plays on the faculty of producing meaning and difference, is more radical than that which plays on labor power.

The *form*-sign must not be confused with the *function* of social differentiation by signs, which, for its part, is contemporaneous with the drama of the bourgeois class, a moneyed class nostalgic for caste values. Since the French moralists of the 17th century, there has been a long literature on the social psychology of distinction and prestige that is connected with the consolidation of the bourgeoisie as a class and that today is generalized to all the middle classes and the petty bourgeoisies. (This literature finds its philosophical resonance in the "dialectic" of being and appearance.) The important question is not this one but rather that of the symbolic destruction of all social relations not so much by the ownership of the means of production but by *the control of the code*. Here there is a revolution of the capitalist system equal in importance to the industrial revolution. And it would be absurd to say that this logic of the sign concerns only the ruling class or the middle class which is "hungry for distinction," the proletariat being free of it thanks to the materiality of its practice. This would be like saying that the theory of the form-commodity was good for the industrial and urban classes, but that the peasants and artisans (the vast majority in Marx's day) had nothing to do with it. The form-sign applies to the whole social process and it is largely unconscious. One must not confuse it with the *conscious* psychology of prestige and differentiation, just as one must not confuse the form-commodity, the abstract and general structure of exchange value, with the *conscious* psychology of profit and economic calculation (where classical political economy remains).

Against those who, fortified behind their legendary materialism, cry idealism as soon as one speaks of signs, or anything that goes beyond manual, productive labor, against those who have a muscular and energetic vision of exploitation, we say that if the term "materialist" has a meaning (one that is critical, not religious) it is we who are the materialists. But it does not matter. Happy are those who cast longing eyes at Marx as if he were always there to give them recognition. What we are attempting to see here is to what point Marxist logic can be rescued from the limited context of political economy in which it arose, so as to account for *our* contradictions. This is on the condition that it give to its theoretical *curvature* the flexibility that it lost long ago in favor of an instrumentalism, of a fixed linearity. We are attempting to rescue it from the limited dimensions of a Euclidean geometry of history in order to test its possibility of becoming what it perhaps is, a truly *general* theory. Once again, this is only an exploratory hypothesis. It postulates a dialectical continuity between the political economy of the commodity and the political economy of the sign (hence of the critique of the one and of the other). The guarantee of this continuity, properly speaking, is not the Marxist postulate of the mode of production. The radical hypothesis no longer accepts this fundamental concept, seeing it as an arbitrary aspect of a certain model. At bottom, the question is posed as follows:

—Are we always within the capitalist mode of production? If the answer is yes, we readily accept classical Marxist analysis.

—Are we within a *later* mode, so different in its structure, in its contradictions and in its mode of revolution, that one must distinguish it radically from capitalism (while maintaining that it is always a question of a mode of production which is determinant as such)?

—Are we, quite simply, within a mode of production at all, and *have we ever been in one?*

Concerning the present phase of political economy, Marxist thought gives us only analyses centered on monopolistic capitalism. In effect, this is the only point which imposes the necessity to theorize something that Marx merely foresaw. But the various theoreticians (Lenin, Rosa Luxemburg, etc.) analyzed it according to the principle of the least theoretical effort, keeping as close as possible to classical concepts and limiting the problem to its infrastructural and political givens (the end of competition, the control of the market, imperialism). But the monopolist stage signifies much more than an extension of the competitive phase of capitalism. It signifies a complete restructuring and a different logic.

What happens when the system becomes monopolistic? In his account in *The Poverty of*

Philosophy, Marx goes back to a citation from
Ricardo: "Commodities which are *monopolized,*
either by an individual, or by a company, vary
according to the law which Lord Lauderdale has
laid down: they fall in proportion as the sellers
augment their quantity, and rise in proportion to the
eagerness of the buyers to purchase them; their price
has no necessary connexion with their natural value;
but the price of commodities, which are subject to
competition, and whose quantity may be increased
in any moderate degree, will ultimately depend, not
on the 'state of demand and supply, but on the
increased or diminished cost of their production."[6]
(Thus, of labor time.) Thus, when the system
becomes monopolistic, labor time and production
costs cease to be the decisive criteria (and become
surplus value?). But one does not go as far with the
law of supply and demand, defined by literal
thought as a *natural* equilibrium of the two terms.
Their correlation is not free, no more than the
market itself. It is the control of demand (Galbraith)
that becomes the strategic articulation. Whereas the
competitive system still acted at a contradictory and
perilous level in the exploitation of labor power, the
monopolistic system transfers its strategy to a level
where the dialectic no longer operates. In the
monopolistic system, there is no longer any dialectic
of supply and demand; this dialectic is short-
circuited by a calculation of foreseeable equilibrium. The monopolistic system (the techno-
structure according to Galbraith) is supported
throughout by a myth of competition,[7] the

6. *The Poverty of Philosophy* (New York: International
Publishers, 1936), p. 42.
7. From this comes the artificial oligopoly on which the real

hegemony of production is supported throughout by a fiction of a dialectic of supply and demand. But there is more to it than this. In the planned cycle of consumer demand, the new strategic forces, the new structural elements — needs, knowledge, culture, information, sexuality — have all their explosive force defused. In opposition to the competitive system, the monopolistic system institutes *consumption* as control, as the abolition of the contingency of demand, as planned socialization by the code (of which advertising, style, etc. are only glaring examples). The contradictions do not end here, but are functionally integrated and neutralized by processes of differentiation and redistribution (processes which the competitive system, in the area of labor power, did not have at its disposal). Thus consumption, which characterizes the monopolistic era, implies something quite different from a phenomenology of affluence: it signifies the passage, by its contradictions, to a mode of strategic control, of predictive anticipation, of the absorption of the dialectic, and of the general homeopathy of the system.

Demand and need correspond more and more to a mode of simulation. These new productive forces no longer pose questions to the system: they are an anticipated response, controlled in their very emergence. The system can afford the luxury of contradiction and dialectic through the play of signs. It can indulge itself with all the signs of revolution. Since it produces all the responses, it annihilates the

monopoly is stablized. Just as bipartisanism is the optimal political form for the functioning of monopoly power by a single class, so peaceful coexistence of two powers (soon three) is the stabilized form of world imperialism.

question in the same blow. Only with the imposition and monopoly of the code is this possible. Whatever one does, one can only respond to the system in its own terms, according to its own rules, answering it with its own signs. the passage to this stage thus constitutes something more than the end of competition. It means that one goes from a system of productive forces, exploitation, and profit, as in the competitive system dominated in its logic by social labor time, to a gigantic operational game of question and answer, to a gigantic combinatory where all values commutate and are exchanged according to their operational sign. The monopolistic stage signifies less the monopoly of the means of production (which is never total) than *the monopoly of the code*.

This stage is accompanied by a radical change in the functioning of the sign, in the *mode of signification*. The finalities of prestige and distinction still corresponded to a traditional status of the sign, in which a signifier referred back to a signified, in which a formal difference, a distinctive opposition (the cut of a piece of clothing, the style of an object) still referred back to what one could call the use value of the sign, to a differential profit, to a lived distinction (a signified value). This is still the classical era of signification with its referential psychology (and philosophy). It is also the *competitive* era in the manipulation of signs. The form-sign describes an entirely different organization: the signified and the referent are now abolished to the sole profit of the play of signifiers, of a generalized formalization in which the code no longer refers back to any subjective or objective "reality," but to its own logic. The signifier becomes its own referent and the use value of the

sign disappears to the benefit of its commutation
and exchange value alone. The sign no longer designates anything at all. It approaches its true
structural limit which is to refer back only to other
signs. All reality then becomes the place of a semi-
urgical manipulation, of a structural simulation.
And, whereas the traditional sign (also in linguistic
exchanges) is the object of a conscious investment, of
a rational calculation of signifieds, here it is the code
that becomes the instance of absolute reference,
and, at the same time, the object of a perverse
desire.[8]

There is a total homology with the sphere of the
commodity. The "traditional" commodity (up to the
era of competitive capitalism) is at once exchange
value and real use value. The proper and final
relation of the subject with the produced object, the
consumptive finality of the product, still exists, just
as the use value of the signified in the classical
organization of the sign. Already there is a general
equivalence of production (the abstraction of
exchange value), but not a general equivalence of
consumption since the products maintain a concrete
finality. With monopolistic capitalism, the same
mutation occurs in the sphere of the sign; the final
reference of the products, their use value,
completely disappears. Needs lose all their autonomy; they are coded. Consumption no longer has a
value of enjoyment per se; it is placed under the
constraint of an absolute finality which is that of
production. Production, on the contrary, is no
longer assigned any finality other than itself. This
total reduction of the process to a single one of its

8. Cf. Baudrillard, "Fétishisme et idéologie," *Nouvelle revue
de psychanalyse* 2 (Fall, 1970).

terms, in which the others are only excuses (use value is the excuse for exchange value; the referent is the excuse for the code) designates more than an evolution of the capitalist mode: it is a mutation. Through the elevation of production to a total abstraction (production for its own sake), to the power of a code, *which no longer even risks being called into question by an abolished referent*, the system succeeds in neutralizing not only consumption, but production itself as a field of contradictions. Productive forces as a referent ("objective" substance of the production process) and thus also as a revolutionary referent (motor of the contradictions of the mode of production) lose their specific impact, and the dialectic no longer operates between productive forces and relations of production, just as the "dialectic" no longer operates between the substance of signs and the signs themselves.[9]

Contradiction and Subversion: The Displacement of the Political

With the generalization of political economy, it becomes more and more evident that its first principle is not in the exploitation of labor as a productive force, where Marxist analysis examined it, but in the imposition of a form, of a general code of rational abstraction, in which capitalist rationalization of material production is only a particular case. The domestication of language in the code of

9.   Economically, this process culminates in the virtual international autonomy of finance capital, in the uncontrollable play of floating capital. Once currencies are extracted from all productive cautions, and even from all reference to the gold standard, general equivalence becomes the strategic place of the manipulation. Real production is everywhere subordinated to it. This apogee of the system corresponds to the triumph of the code.

signification, the domestication of all social and symbolic relations in the schema of representation, are not only contemporary with political economy, *they are its very process*. And it is here, in these "superstructural" realms today that it presents its form and radicalizes itself. The capitalist system, tied to profit and to exploitation, is only the inaugural modality, the infantile phase of the system of political economy. The schema of value (exchange and use) and of general equivalence is no longer limited to the area of "production": it has permeated the spheres of language, of sexuality, etc. The form has not changed (hence one can speak of a political economy of the sign, of a political economy of the body, *without metaphor*). But the center of gravity has been displaced; the epicenter of the contemporary system is no longer the process of material production.

This is not to say that, at bottom, the political economy of language, of the sign, of representation did not begin well before that of material production. If the quantitative operationalization of productive forces has been able to serve, for nearly two centuries, as the fundamental reference, this is perhaps only an apparent movement. For a much longer period, the operationalization of the code has been fundamental (division, abstraction, functional systematization and structural arrangement). It is this that unfolds today in all its consequences. But it is not a matter of changing the determinant instance and reversing the priorities: this would be a regression to a naive idealism that privileges the contents of representation whereas a naive materialism privileges the contents of production. There is nothing to choose between these two alternatives. The system itself does not present this difficulty: it comprises neither materialism nor idealism, nor infrastructure nor superstructure. It proceeds according to its form and this form carries along all of them at the same time: production and representation, signs and commodities, language and labor power. It is its own determination in the last instance. It is on this form that today is inscribed, at all levels, terror and social abstraction.

The truly capitalist phase of forced socialization through labor and the intensive mobilization of productive forces has been overturned. We have now a *desublimation of productive forces*, not by the lessening of the contradictions between the logic of the system and the world, but, on the contrary, through its logical process of expanded reproduction. Everything happens as if industrial coercion, disciplined concentration, the more and more extensive integration of the masses in the apparatus of production since the 19th century, the planned crystallization of all energies into material production were only a provisional solution, gigantic but temporary, for a project of rationalization and social control whose scope largely overcomes this phase. Surplus value, profit, exploitation—all these "objective realities" of capital have no doubt worked to mask the immense social domestication, the immense controlled sublimation of the process of production, appearing only as the *tactical* side of the process. The system is reproduced today through a reverse tactic: no longer one of general mobilization, but of techno-structural rationalization, that has as its effect the corruption of all the categories, or rather, a greater and greater fraction of the productive social time of all categories. It is no longer in the sphere of productive exploitation, but in the "demobilized," the repressively "desubli-

mated" sphere, in relation to production, that the
contradictions today emerge.

After forced industrialization and direct exploitation come prolonged education, studies subsidized
for twenty-five years, endless personal development,
and recycling: everything is apparently destined to
multiply and differentiate social productivity. In
fact, the system needs this sophistication, this versa-
tility, this truly unlimited personal development, but
only for a statistically limited group at a very high
social level. At most, it is achieved by a very mobile
group of versatile technocrats who assume all
decision-making functions, and by a mass of disqualified persons, who are on their own and socially
irresponsible while having the illusion of participation and personal growth.[10] All the institutions
of "advanced democracy," all "social conquests"
concerning growth, culture, personal and collective
creativity, all of this is, as it has always been, simply
the right of private property, the real right of the
few. And for everyone else there are day-care centers
and nurseries, institutions of social control in which
the productive forces are deliberately neutralized.
For the system no longer needs universal productivity; it requires only that everyone play the game.

This leads to the paradox of social groups who are
compelled to fight for a place in the circuit of work
and of productivity, the paradox of generations who
are left out or placed off limits by the very
development of the productive forces. The reverse of
capitalism's initial situation.[11] From this circum-

---

10. This division is already in effect at the level of the
grandes écoles and the universities.

11. For example, in the United States the establishment of
an indefinite salary-unemployment that neutralizes entire groups
as producers while maintaining them as consumers. It is no

stance new contradictions are born. For if the exploited class bore a violent contradiction it was still in the order of an integration, of a socialization, brutal and forced, but nevertheless one of socialization in the order of the general productive system. Revolt emerged against the integration of labor power as a factor of production. The new social groups, de facto dropouts, on the contrary, proved the incapacity of the system to "socialize the society" in its traditionally strategic level, to dynamically integrate them, even by violent contradiction at the level of production. And it is on the basis of their *total irresponsibility* that these marginal generations carry on the revolt. This revolt can remain ambiguous if it is experienced as anomie and as defeat, if it occupies by default the marginal position assigned to it by the system or if it is institutionalized as marginal. But it is enough that it radically adopts this forced exteriority to the system in order to call the system into question, no longer as functioning in the interior but from the exterior, as a fundamental structure of the society, as a code, as a culture, as an interiorized social space. The whole system of production would then be disinvested; it would teeter on this social void that it itself produced. All its positivity would crumble on this non-place, on this disaffected zone and those who are left alone would return their total disaffection to the system. Subversion is born there, an *elsewhere*,

---

longer a question of the strategy of "the reserve army of capital," but of testing everyone and, as in school (this society puts everyone in school) of having ready and available (at a cost of enormous financial "sacrifices," but who does not make them for the reproduction of the system?) a whole social group who becomes the idle and parasitic clients of the system. There is no longer savage exploitation but tutellage and exile.

whereas contradiction operates at the *interior* of the system.[12]

Hence there is a major role for students, youth who are disqualified in advance, voluntarily or not, as well as all types of social groups, of regional communities, ethnic or linguistic, because, by the process of the centralization and technocratic pyramidalization of the system, they fall into marginality, into the periphery, into the zone of disaffection and irresponsibility. Excluded from the game, their revolt henceforth aims at the rules of the game. Desocialized, they defeat the capitalist social *reality principle*, and not merely their exploitation by the system. Segregated, discriminated against, satellitized—they are gradually relegated *to a position of non-marked terms* by the structuration of the system as a code. Their revolt thus aims at the abolition of this code, this strategy composed of distinction, separations, discriminations, oppositions that are structured and hierarchized.

The Black revolt aims at race as a code, at a level much more radical than economic exploitation. The revolt of women aims at the code that makes the feminine a non-marked term. The youth revolt aims at the extremity of a process of racist discrimination in which it has no right to speak. The same holds for all those social groups that fall under the structural bar of repression, of relegation to a place where they lose their meaning. This position of revolt is no longer that of the economically exploited; it aims

---

12. But we can always ask if this demobilization, this virtual lockout, answers the secret demands of the calculation of productivity, hence of the system itself in its reproduction (since it goes so far as to finance unproductive marginality) or if it constitutes, through disinvestment and growing defection, a model of subversion.

less at the extortion of surplus value than at the imposition of the code, which inscribes the present strategy of social domination.

The more the system becomes concentrated, the more it expels whole social groups. The more it becomes hierarchized according to the law of value (sign or commodity) the more it excludes whoever resists this law. So it was that madness was confined (Michel Foucault) at the threshold of Western rationality. Today it is the same for all civil society, which has become a place of confinement where tranquillized man is closely watched. Everywhere behind the factory and the school, the suburb or the office, the museum or the hospital, it is the asylum and the ghetto that are profiled as the purest form of a truly rationalized society.

This terrorist rationality has produced, in the course of centuries, the radical distinction of the masculine and the feminine with the "racial" inferiorization and sexual objectification of the feminine. No culture but ours has produced this systematic abstraction in which all the elements of symbolic exchange between the sexes have been liquidated to the profit of a binary functionality. And this separation, which has taken on all of its force with capitalist political economy, is not reabsorbed at the present time. Sexual hyperactivism, equalization of the sexes, "liberation of desire," in short, the "Sexual Revolution," gives only the illusion of symbolic destructuring under the sign of sex as a differential mark, as an index of status and as a function of pleasure. It is this mark that the women's revolt (or the gay liberation) aims at, not the claims, democratic and rationalist, of political or sexual rights to equality (the equivalent of the salary claims of the worker). Not the accession of women to power, that is, the turning of the code to their favor, but the abolition of the code. Marxism has either ignored this subversion of the political economy of sex, that is, the imposition of the law of value in the sexual domain, the imposition of the phallus, the masculine, as the general sexual equivalent, or else it has "dialectically" subordinated it to economic contradictions, allowing all of its radicality to escape.

The same observations hold for racial discrimination. No other culture besides ours has produced the systematic distinction of Black and White. And this distinction applies not as an afterthought but as a structural element which is reproduced ever more dynamically today under the appearances of faltering liberal universalism. And the objectification of the Black as such is not that of exploited labor power, but an objectification by the *code*. One can easily verify that it is sustained by a whole arsenal of significations, irreducible to economic and political determinations. The emancipated or embourgeoisified Black remains a Black, just as the proletarianized immigrant remains first of all an immigrant, as the Jew remains a Jew. Again the code re-emerges with more violence in everything that would seem to suppress it. In Marxist terms, the superstructure is imposed with more force as the contradictions connected to the infrastructure are resolved, which is to say the least, paradoxical. Here again, the autonomization of the Black as the principle of revolution, as well as the autonomization of women as sex or of the proletariat as class, only renews the racial or sexual code, the game of political economy, simply by displacing the marked term.

The other form of discrimination against youth is not at all a secondary effect of class domination or economic exploitation, but the most explosive consequence of the present system. The hierarchical monopoly over decision-making circumscribes more and more under the zero term of social significance. Youth occupies the most critical non-place of the code, but not as an age group. If its revolt has repercussions everywhere, it is because this non-place crosses all social categories. In the economy, in politics, in science and in culture, today it is irresponsibility that is crucial. It is a revolt of those who have been pushed aside, who have never been able to speak or have their voices heard.

Speech itself is defined as an incessant response (responsibility), in which all social transcendence is dissolved. Against the spoken word, political economy, throughout its history, supports *discourse* in which everything that is exchanged is put under the instance of the code. At the side of all the discriminations, the markings and demarkings of which we have spoken, the system produced a fundamental separation of the signifier from signified. Through it and the whole logic of communications that it institutes, the system has succeeded, slowly but inexorably, in neutralizing the symbolic power of the spoken word. Binary structuring, the abstraction of representational discourse, the general equivalent and foreclosure of the code—these are the elements of the logic of the system.[13] The insurrectional practice of the past few years has given new voice to

---

13. Linguistics and semiology administer, by "scientific" analyses, this social exclusion of the spoken word. They defend the code because in its the life and death of the system is played out not in a sensational way, but in a political way nonetheless.

the spoken word and eclipses traditional contradictions.

These revolts do not profile class struggle. But
capitalism and its weakness evolve. Buried until now
under the "determinant instance" of the mode of
production, they surface according to the logic of
the expanded reproduction of the system. The
ethnic and linguistic minorities, repressed and en-
slaved in the thread of history by bureaucratic centralization; the oppression of women, children,
youth, also the elderly; the whole cycle of repression
and adjustment organized within the nuclear family
as the structure of the reproduction of the order of
production; polymorphous, non-genital, "perverse"
sexuality, liquidated or submerged by the genital
principle of sexual reality; nature as a productive
force subjected to total spoilation — in these cases
and in others the process of capitalism crosses the
entire network of natural, social, sexual and cultural
forces, all languages and codes. In order to function,
capitalism needs to dominate nature, to domesticate
sexuality, to rationalize language as a means of
communication, to relegate ethnic groups, women,
children and youth to genocide, ethnocide and
racial discrimination. One must not see here, as in
rigid Marxism, simple excrescences or even attempts
at diversion from the fundamental theme that still
would remain as always the "class struggle." In this
doctrinaire confusion there is a mystification of
Marxist thought which, by circumscribing the
economy as the fundamental determination, allows
mental, sexual, and cultural structures to function
efficaciously. But, if capitalism has, through the
centuries, played on all the "superstructural" ideologies in order to let the steam out of economic con-

traditions today the strategy is reversed. The system now plays on the economic reference (well-being, consumption, but also working conditions, salaries, productivity, growth) as an alibi against the more serious subversion that threatens it in the symbolic order. It is the economic sphere, with its partial contradictions that today acts as an ideological factor of integration. By making itself an accomplice of this diversion, Marxism is very simply exploited by capitalism as a force in ideological labor (spontaneous and benevolent). Everything that today gives priority to the economic field in salary claims or theorizing the economy as the last instance (Séguy or Althusser) is "objectively" idealist and reactionary.

The radical subversion is *transversal* to the extent that it crosses the contradictions connected with the mode of production, and *non-dialectical* to the extent that there is no dialectical negativity in the relation between a repressed, non-marked term and a marked term. There can only be transgression of the line and deconstruction of the code.[14] This subversion telescopes "traditional" contradictions. But they do not converge since they are separated by a strategic mutation of the system. A conjuncture of the working class and the students (or, the idle young and the workers) under the pious invocation of a common exploitation is impossible. The respective demands diverge, and they diverge more and more despite the desperate efforts of the student and Leftist movement in "politicizing" their subversion by an immersion in the working class. On the one

---

14. But one can also aim to simply pass to the other side of the line in order to become the marked term, to change positions without breaking the code: The "White" Black man, etc.

hand are the workers who obstinately defend, on the basis of the salary system and their integration in the industrial system, their "right to work" and the advantages the system yields them.[15] On the other are the Leftists, the social groups (of sex, age, race, ethnicity, language, culture, knowledge — all "superstructural" criteria that are historically overcome according to the rationalist perspective of the class struggle) who are demobilized, demarked, excluded, and in whom the ethic of the system crumbles. Between these two forces the gap grows larger and cannot be bridged. The working class is no longer the gold standard of revolts and contradictions. There is no longer a revolutionary subject of reference. The hope to dialecticize, to articulate a subversive movement which calls the system into question as code, as a total language of repression and separation, together with the class contradictions that call the system into question as a mode of production and exploitation, is simply part of the reveries of political voluntarism.

However, something else appears at the very level of the production process. Here also a secret defection lurks and expands as the ulcer of capitalism. Everywhere the work ethic, the secular "instinct of workmanship," the ethic of individual and collective sublimation of the labor process (paradoxically reactivated today by the unions and the "workers' party") are dislocated. One sees (in May, 1968, "Never Work," but also in strikes at Fiat, at Usinor with its strike for the sake of striking, without bread and butter demands) practices

---

15. Until now they appear archaic in front of technocratic reformism: choice of work schedule, job enrichment, anti-assembly line. The unions resist innovation perhaps justly, but on a conservative basis.

emerge that not only deny exploitation, but work itself as the principle of reality and rationality, as *axiomatic*. It is no longer then a question of an internal, dialectical negativity in the mode of production, but a refusal, pure and simple, of production as the general axiomatic of social relations. Without any doubt, the refusal is hidden in salary and corporativist demands; in midstream it is transposed into a carefully asphyxiated and channeled radical[16] denegation by the Parties and the unions, for whom, just as for the system itself, economic demands are the ideal means of control and manipulation. This is what gives the new left or hippie movement its meaning. Not the open revolt of a few, but the immense, latent defection, the endemic, masked resistance of a silent majority, but one nostalgic for the spoken word and for violence. Something in all men profoundly rejoices in seeing a car burn. (In this sense, youth is only the exponential category of a latent process in the entire social expanse, without exception for age or "objective" condition.) On the other hand, the new left commits suicide if it pretends to have statistical significance, to become a mass "political" force. Here it is irremediably lost at the level of representation and of traditional political contradiction (the same holds true for the American counter-culture).

Political Revolution and "Cultural" Revolution

During the last hundred years, capitalism has been able to prevent serious social and political changes by absorbing contradictions when they were posed only at the level of material production. Contradition only becomes radical when, as is the case

---

16. This would mean that traditional contradictions no longer have any apparent meaning. But perhaps they never had?

today, it reaches a level of total social relations. It is by expanding the field of social abstraction to the level of consumption, signification, information and knowledge, by expanding its jurisdiction and control to the whole field of culture and daily life, even to the unconscious, that the system has resolved the partial contradictions connected with economic relations of production. Through a restoration that has taken a century to accomplish, capitalism, by radicalizing its own logic, also has succeeded in radically altering the Marxist definitions of contradiction and revolution.

The "cultural revolution," which corresponds to the radicalized logic of capital, to "in depth" imperialism,[17] is not the developed form of all economic-political revolution. It acts on the basis of a reversal of "materialist" logic. Against the materialist postulate according to which the mode of production and the reproducion of social relations are subordinated to relations of material production, one can ask if it is not the *production* of social relations that determiens the mode of material *reproduction* (the development of productive forces and relations of production). A genealogy of social relations shows many criteria of domination other than the private ownership of the means of production. Species, race, sex, age, language, culture, signs of either an anthropological or cultural type—all these criteria are criteria of *difference,* of signification and of code. It is a simplistic hypothesis that makes them all "descendants" in the last instance of economic exploitation.

---

17. The economic and political planetary extension of capitalism is only the "extensive" modality of this deepening of capital. Moreover, it is to this level that the analysis of "imperialism" is in general limited.

On the contrary, it is truer to say that this hypothesis is itself only the rationalization of an order of domination reproduced through it. A domination that plays the economic as a tactic, a detour and an alibi. Today the essential fact is no longer profit or exploitation. *Perhaps it was never so even in the Golden Age and Iron Age of capitalism.*

It is directly at the level of the production of social relations that capitalism is vulnerable and en route to perdition. Its fatal malady is not its incapacity to reproduce itself economically and politically, but its incapacity to reproduce itself *symbolically*. The symbolic social relation is the uninterrupted cycle of giving and receiving, which, in primitive exchange, includes the consumption of the "surplus" and deliberate anti-production whenever accumulation (the thing not exchanged, taken and not returned, earned and not wasted, produced and not destroyed), risks breaking the reciprocity and begins to generate power. It is this symbolic relation that the political economy model (of capital), whose only process is that of the law of value, hence of appropriation and indefinite accumulation, *can no longer produce*. It is its radical negation. What is produced is no longer symbolically exchanged and what is not symbolically exchanged (the commodity) feeds a social relation of power and exploitation.

It is this fatality of symbolic disintegration under the sign of economic rationality that capitalism cannot escape. One can also say, with Cardan, that its fundamental contradiction is no longer between the development of productive forces and relations of production, but in the impossibility of having people "participate." However, the term "participation" has a connotation that is much too contractual and rationalist to express the nature of

the symbolic. Let us say that the system is
structurally incapable of liberating human potentials except as *productive* forces, that is, according to
an operational finality that leaves no room for the
reversion of the loss, the gift, the sacrifice and hence
for the possibility of symbolic exchange.

The example of consumption is significant. The
feudal system died because it could not find the path
to rational productivity. The bourgeoisie knew how
to make the people work, but it also narrowly
escaped destruction in 1929 because it did not know
how to make them consume. It was content, until
then, to socialize people by force and exploit them
through labor. But the crisis in 1929 marked the
point of asphyxiation: the problem was no longer
one of production but one of circulation.
Consumption became the strategic element; the
people were henceforth mobilized as consumers;
their "needs" became as essential as their labor
power. By this operation, the system assured its
economic survival at a fantastically expanded level.
But something else is at play in the strategy of consumption. By allowing for the possibility of
expanding and consuming, by organizing social redistribution (social security, allotments, salaries that
are no longer defined as the strict economic
reproduction of labor power) by launching advertising, human relations, etc., the system created the
illusion of a symbolic participation (the illusion that
something that is taken and won is also redistri-
buted, given, and sacrificed). In fact, this entire
symbolic simulation is uncovered as leading to super-
profits and super-power. In spite of all its good will
(at least among those capitalist who are aware of the
necessity of tempering the logic of the system in
order to avoid an explosion in the near future), it

cannot make consumption a true *consummation*, a festival, a waste. To consume is to start producing again. All that is expended is in fact invested; nothing is ever totally lost. Even when coffee stocks burn, when enormous wealth is squandered in war, the system cannot stop having this lead to a widening reproduction. It is caught in the necessity of producing, accumulating, making a profit. Its assistance to developing countries is returned in multiple profits. Even if the liberal experts denounce, as they have for twenty years, the catastrophe that will come at the end of this process, the rich nations cannot reduce (even if they clearly wanted to), at the cost of *real* sacrifices, the gulf that separates them from the Third World. And this also means that each individual, each consumer, is locked into the profitable manipulation of goods and signs for his own interest. He can no longer really *waste his time* in leisure.[18] Inexorably, he reproduces, at his own level, the whole system of political economy: the logic of appropriation, the impossibility of waste, of the gift, of loss, the inexorability of the law of value.

There is the same conjuncture at the political level. Power consists in the monopoly of the spoken word; the spoken word (decision, responsibility) is no longer exchanged. But this situation is explosive; those who have power know it. And we see them desperately attempting to divest themselves of a portion of the spoken word, of redistributing a part of the responsibilities in order to avoid a boomerang of the kind that occurred in May, 1968. But they *cannot do it*. They would like to have participation, but participation is revealed each time as being only

---

18. Cf. Baudrillard, *La société de consommation* (Paris: Denoël, 1970).

a better tactic for the wider reproducton of the system. The more autonomy is given to everyone, the more decision-making is concentrated at the summit.19 Just as in 1929, when the system almost died from an inability to circulate production, so today it is perishing from an inability to circulate the spoken word. Because it is a system of production, it can only reproduce itself. It can no longer achieve any symbolic integration (the reversibility of the process of accumulation in festivals and waste, the reversibility of the process of production in destruction, the reversibility of the process of power in exchange and death).

At all levels, the system is sick from desublimation, from liberalization, from tolerance, while seeking to transcend itself in order to survive. Consumption, satisfaction of needs, sexual liberation, women's rights, etc., etc. — it is prepared to grant anything in order to reduce social abstraction so that people will play the game. But it cannot do it, once again, because this liberalization is only hyper-repressive. Needs which were once contingent and heterogeneous are homogenized and definitively rationalized according to the models of the system. Sexuality, which was once repressed, is liberated as a game of signs. It objectifies sexuality as the functionality of the body and the profitability of the pleasure principle. Information is liberated, but only in order to be better managed and stylized by the media. Everywhere the pressure of the system of political economy is heightened. The final avatars are anti-pollution and job enrichment. Here also the

---

19.   The autonomy of the faculties is, as we know, the best means of aligning them with capitalist productivity, just as the independence of colonial nations was the best means of perpetuating and modernizing their exploitation.

system seems to slacken its limits and restore nature and work in their dignity: a desublimation of productive forces in relation to traditional exploitation. But we know very well that a symbolic relation of man to nature or to his work will not re-emerge here. There will only be a more flexible and reinforced operationality of the system.

We are faced with coding, super-coding, universalization of the code, proliferating axiomatization of the capitalist system (Deleuze). But against the triumphant abstraction, against the irreversible monopolization, the demand arises that nothing can be given without being returned, nothing is ever won without something being lost, nothing is ever produced without something being destroyed, nothing is ever spoken without being answered. In short, what haunts the system is the symbolic demand.

The Economic as Ideology and Simulation Model

Against subversion by the symbolic, which to some degree arises under the label "cultural revolution," the capitalist system has every interest in diverting it through "closetting" the contradictions within the economic realm. Autonomizing the economic is an ideological strategy. Bourdieu describes [20] the same phenomenon in relation to scholarly and cultural systems. The scholarly and cultural systems are permitted to have formal autonomy (which is theorized as transcendence and is presented as a democratic and universal truth—equality of instruction and culture for each—while class structure is reversed for the order of production). It is through this autonomy effect and behind this simulacrum of

---

20. *La réproduction* (Paris: Minuit, 1970).

transcendence that the system better carries out its ideological function and renews most efficaciously the dominant social relations. One can ask if it serves only to reproduce them and if it is not the place of a *specific production* of class domination. For this implies a reversal of the terms of analysis: the economic can appear in our societies as the most important place of the equalization of opportunity, of the least conservatism of social relations, etc. (historically, since the appearance of the bourgeoisie, the economy has always played the role of the springboard of emancipation as compared to the more conservative juridical, religious, and cultural structures). And perhaps it is the scholarly and cultural systems that play the decisive role in the *production* of social relations, while the economic only relays and shifts them in their *reproduction*.

In any case, the ideological process, as it emerges in Bourdieu's analysis, has not changed and it can be generalized as follows: ideology always proceeds by an autonomization of a partial totality; all autonomized partial totalities immediately have an ideological value. This is the way Bourdieu treats the scholarly system. But *all* partial fields, in particular the economic, can, for the same reason, act as ideological fields, once erected as an autonomous instance (and even determinant). But the autonomization of the economic sphere is common to capitalism and to Marxism.

1. All autonomized partial social fields become, at the same time, the place of a universalist and egalitarian myth: religion was in its time; scholarly and cultural systems are today; consumption as a function isolated from production is rapidly becoming one. But the economic sphere affirms itself in its autonomy when faced with the religious,

the cultural, etc., as the sphere of social *rationality*, as the *universal* instance of productivity (here again the Marxists are no different from the bourgeois economists), and thus as an egalitarian myth. Each is equal in rights before the objective reason of production.

2. The economic sphere is supported by science. For all detached fields as such secrete a myth of rigor, of objectivity, of truth. Objectivity and truth are only the *effect* of the parcellization of a field of knowledge, of its autonomization under certain rules. Being closed off from everything else by a perfect and fragmented knowledge, that is the imaginary of the exact sciences, and the desire of science is nothing but the fascination with miscomprehension. Political economy as a science of the detached is thus properly ideological and the critique of political economy, when it wishes itself to be "scientific" (materialist), only serves to reinforce its object as a detached abstraction. There are no economic truths, or better, we have fashioned the truth of the economic as an arbitrary instance.

3. All partial fields, including the economic, are the fields of contradiction which are also partial. The place of the fundamental contradiction—the place of politics today—is the line of separation between the partial fields. And revolution is not the resolution of partial contradictions, but the abolition of this line. The internal contradictions in the partial fields are the echo of the separation that haunts them. It is their point of origin. They are thus ambiguous: at the same time that they manifest an obsession with non-separation, they reinforce the separations by autonomizing them as *internal* contradictions. Their resolution can never go beyond the separation, which is why it is never final.

They are resolved in a flight from the partial system under the obsession with separation (others would say with castration). Such is the process of political economy; such is the *imaginary* of political economy (Cardan).

The whole materialist critique of ideology, the denunciation of the autonomization of the values of consciousness, of culture, of the simulation of a reality principle of ideas, this whole critique *is turned back against materialism in an integral way*, that is, against the autonomization of the economic insofar as it is a (determinant) instance.

The economic appears everywhere as the theorization of the rupture with symbolic exchange, as the institution of a detached field that then becomes the vector of a total reorganization of social life. It is the simulation of a universal finality of calculation and productive rationality, the simulation of a *determination* whereas symbolic exchange knows of neither determination nor end. It is the simulation of a *reality* of this instance, of an economic reality principle that goes on to universalize itself on the basis of the very principle of separation. Today this *model* is found in its completed form with operational models, with the simulation of situations having the purpose of prediction and control, with operational artifacts replacing reality and the code of the reality principle.[21]

Cardan says, "The rationality of modern society is only in its form: it is the syllogism of growth, camouflaged as the historical dialectic of the

---

21. Thus idealist simulation and materialist simulation are joined. Their common schema is the separation of instances under the jurisdiction of one of them (the same schema as in the semiological reduction). Cf. *Nouvelle revue de psychanalyse, op.cit.*

development of productive forces. But in this syllogism, the premises borrow their content from the imaginary. And the prevalence of the syllogism as such, the obsession with a rationality detached from everything else, constitutes an imaginary to the second degree. Modern pseudo-rationality is a form of the imaginary in history. It is arbitrary in its ultimate ends as long as these ends do not reveal any rationality. And it is arbitrary when it posits itself as end (this holds for logical reason and for "dialectical" reason). In this respect, the modern world is prey to a systematic delirium, of which the autonomization of unfettered technology (and bureaucracy) is the most immediately perceptible and menacing form... The economy exhibits, in the most striking fashion, the domination of the imaginary at all levels."

The symbolic is the abolition of the imaginary of political economy (and of all other detached fields). In this sense, the cultural revolution is no longer tied to the economic-political revolution. It cuts through the economic-political as a partial revolutionary discourse and, in a certain rationalizing and mystifying way. A revolution that aims at the totality of life and social relations will be made also and primarily against the autonomization of the economic, of which the last ("revolutionary" and materialist) avatar is the autonomization of the mode of production under the form of a determinant instance. Because today the system has no better strategy than that of the dialectic of political economy, the cultural revolution must make itself against the economic-political revolution.

Marxist Theory and the Workers' Movement:
The Concept of Class

This revolutionary potentiality, this subversion directed against the axiomatic of productive rationality itself (including its internal contradictions) is no longer accounted for by a Marxist analysis of class and mode of production. Marxism is incapable of theorizing *total* social practice (including the most radical form of Marxism) except to reflect it in the mirror of the mode of production. It cannot lead to the dimensions of a revolutionary "politics." From our current position, Marxist analysis, in its revolutionary rationality, no longer illuminates either modern societies or primitive societies.

Retrospectively, moreover, it is necessary to ask *if it has not always been thus*, if already in Marx's time the theory of the mode of production did not effect an extraordinary simplification of social practice. If it no longer accounts for the present mode of revolution, did it, at least for a given moment of history (the "classical" capitalist phase) account for fundamental contradictions? Did the mode of production (and with it class and class struggle) have its hour of truth?

The sacrilegious hypothesis is here imposed that the conjuncture in the 19th century of Marxist theory and the workers' movement perhaps had not been the miracle of history—the greatest event in history, says Althusser—*but a process of reciprocal reduction and neutralization*. The objective historical result was the choking of both in the Leninist *political* mixture, later in the Stalinist bureaucracy, and today in the most vulgar reformist empiricism. These are the stages of a long decline that it would be too simple to impute to a few distortions along the way. The deep logic of this decline forces us to return beyond Stalin, beyond Lenin, etc., back to the crucial point of the thought of Marx himself, back to the original event, which is always conceived as irrevocably revolutionary, of the dialectical conjuncture of his theory and the objective social practice of a class called the proletariat. We have so lived in the providential shadow of this event that the idea that this fusion was not necessary, nor necessarily the best, has never truly been formulated. Social revolt and the movement of the theory, each indexing themselves on the other, each *verifying* themselves in the thread of history, were universalized as historical reason, under the sign of the dialectical revolution. But they were lost as society's radical difference.

In effect, the fusion was not made between a radical revolt and a radical theory, both of them "primitive" and non-determined (as was the case in the insurrectional movements of the 19th century up to the Commune of 1871 and again in May, 1968) but between two terms that were already distinct and slanted by each other. If you wish, this is dialectical but it is necessary to see that what is dialecticized, that upon which Marxist theory hinges, is a social reality "specified" as a class, as an objective and conscious organization, as a proletariat. What is grasped in theory as proletarian organization is a well-determined social critique in terms of a mode of production, relations of production and class. On one side there is an "objective" and organized class and on the other side there is a rational and structured theory (as much in its materialist content as in its dialectical form)—it is between these two terms, each rationalized in the image of the other, that the dialectic of revolution has been short-circuited. It is difficult to evaluate all that has been repressed and eliminated in this operation which brings out once and forever, under the sign of materialism, history, and the dialectic, the *revolutionary reality principle*. Let us say that everything that a "pleasure principle" and a radicality of revolt would reveal and can still be read in the insurrectionists of the 19th century, in the destruction of machines, in pre-Marxist utopian and libertarian discourse, in the cursed poets or in the sexual revolt, and that aimed, well beyond material production, at a total symbolic configuration of life and social relations is destroyed by the abstract configuration of political economy — that it is this whole primitive and radical movement that Marxist *theory* and socialist *organization*, in their miraculous conjunction, have dialecticized by treating it, under a class status and a "historical" content, as the development of productive forces. They rationalized it into a relation of antagonistic forces *at the interior* of a single social field, magnetized by political economy.

But this revolt implied something different from a *dialectic of forces*. It implied the irruption of a radical *difference,* something far different from surplus value and the exploitation of labor power which is the corruption of all social relations by the unilateral rationality of production and universal socialization under the law of value. And the operation, if one looks at it closely, consisted in a "dialectical" rehabilitation of the status of the producer, towards which the revolt aimed, and of which Marxist theory itself made the point of departure of the social revolution. Marxism makes a revolutionary detour and a promise of liberation out of a process of destructuring and repression.

(Nietzsche is right: the workers have elevated into a cardinal value the very sign of their slavery, just as the Christians did with suffering.) And this revolution is no longer for the here and now: it becomes a historical finality. Positivized under the sign of progress by the bourgeoisie, or dialecticized under the sign of revolution by Marxism, it is always the case of an imposition of a meaning, the rational projection of an objective finality opposing itself to the radicality of desire which, in its non-meaning, cuts through all finality.

In relation to the situation created by massive industrialization, concentration-camp discipline, the rigid training of generations of artisans and peasants beginning in the 19th century, in relation to the situation of destructuring and revolt, Marxist theory and workers' organization have achieved overall a labor of historical rationalization, a certain kind of *secondary elaboration*: the valorization of labor as the source of social wealth, the valorization of the process of the rational development of productive forces, a *process* that was confused with the revolutionary *project* (surely through a "dialectical" negativity, but behind which was hidden irrevocably the confusion of this same class with labor as the social ethic of class).

The ethic of rational labor, which is of bourgeois origin and which served historically to define the bourgeoisie as a class, is found renewed with fantastic amplitude at the level of the working class, also contributing *to define* it as a class, that is to circumscribe it in a status of historical representability.

Respect for the machine, protection for work instruments, implying virtual propriety (some kind of human right in opposition to legal right) and the future appropriation of the means of production, institutes the working class in a productivist vocation that takes the place of the historic vocation of the bourgeoisie. The fact that in the revolutionary project these means of production are restored to the disposition of those who produce, under the sign of social appropriation and self-management, only gives an eternal quality to the process of production, beyond all changes in the mode of production. The "class of laborers" is thus confirmed in its idealized status as a productive force even by its revolutionary ideal. It reflects upon itself as "the most precious human capital," as the myth of origin of social wealth.

In the guise of historical materialism, the idealism of production ends by giving a positive definition to the revolutionary class. The class is then *defined in the universal*, according to the universality of labor power. It falls back upon an essence which in fact it was assigned by the bourgeois class and which defines it, in its historical being, by the universality of capital. Capital and labor power then encounter each other as respective values, equally founded in the universal.[22] In this encounter of classes where each has its objective, historical *reference*, the bourgeois class always prevails. For this concept of class belongs to it and when it succeeds in trapping the proletariat in it, it has already won the game. The concept of class is a universalist and rationalist

---

22.   This confusion is instituted once again by the fact that besides the *exchange value* of labor power — the level of exploitation and dialectical contradiction — Marxist theory preserves a level of the *use value* of labor, a level that is irreducible to the positivity of value, that is, a mirror of a human positivity of labor where the proletarian class, sliding from the negative to the positive, comes to recognize itself. Use value, once again, plays a dirty trick on Marxist theory.

concept, born in a society of rational production and
of the calculation of productive forces. In a sense,
there has always been and there will always be only
one class, the bourgeoisie. This capitalist bourgeois
class is defined not only by the ownership of the
means of production, but by the rational *finality* of
production. To make a class of the proletariat is
hence to enclose it in an order of definition
(characterized by "class consciousness" as "the
subject of history")23 in which the model remains

---

23.   In this regard, the very beautiful dialectic of Lukács in
History and Class Consciousness takes on a totally ambiguous
meaning. The rational vocation of the class as the subject of
history, the articulation of this process through the consciousness
that the class has of itself—in these notions the path is paved for
hypostasizing the being of class, for the triumph of the reality
principle and the representability of the class, hence, really for
the triumph of the Party. At one level this dialectical and
"spontaneous" collective class consciousness seems to contradict
the bureaucratic process (this is why the Stalinists, always super-
ficial, violently attacked it). But at a more profound level, there
is a collusion between a *rationalist* theory of class consciousness
and the formal *rationality* of the bureaucracy. It is no accident
that Lukácsian theory, dialectical and spontaneist, appears at
the moment when the bureaucratic monopoly of the Party was
historically reinforced. It did not object fundamentally to this
process since, fixing a reflected essence, a class rationality, a for-
itself as the subject of history, it necessarily presented a logic of
representation and identification together with an ideal instance
(in some way the "ego ideal" of the class). This instance can only
be the organization and the Party. To the imaginary subject of
history corresponds profoundly the paranoic machine of the
bureaucracy. (In the same way, the idealization of the conscious
subject is contemporary, through all of Western history, with the
extension of rational control by the State. It is the same
operation that rebounds at the level of the class with Lukács.) He
returned to Stalinism to write *The Destruction of Reason* in
order to denounce the irrationality of fascism. But fascism is only
irrational for bourgeois democracy. In fact, it incarnates an
extreme of paranoic Reason, an extreme that "dialectical
Reason" cannot argue against when it falls into the imaginary
transcendence of a subject, of the proletarian class. Upon such
an abstraction one can only build (and with Stalin, logically, will

that of the bourgeoisie. Accession to the status of
class is equivalent to a rationalization of the
"workers' movement" and its revolt, equivalent to
aligning it in the general rationality of the industrial
order. Thus "class against class" can well signify
antagonism at the level of the relation to the *means*
of production, but this in no way breaks the *finality*
of productivity itself. On the contrary, but dialec-
ticizing it from within, this schema serves only to
extend the process of political economy to infinity.

If the class struggle has a meaning, it is not in the
encounter of one class with another. (When the
structure is reversed and the proletarian class
triumphs, as in the East, nothing changes
profoundly, as we know, in social relations.) This
meaning can only be the radical refusal of letting
itself be enclosed in the being and consciousness of
class. For the proletariat, it is to negate the
bourgeoisie because the latter assigns it a class status.
It must not negate itself insofar as it is deprived of
the means of production (which is, unfortunately,
the "objective" Marxist definition of class); it
negates itself insofar as it is defined in terms of
production and political economy. Can the
proletariat have a meaning if it defines itself in terms

---

be built) totalitarianism, that is, the total taking in charge, the
total control of the class by an organizational instance under the
sign of Reason. Class consciousness, that idealist vision, yields
but one mode of objective existence: the Party. It is not class
consciousness, in its own movement, that bestows the Party or
the organization as the dialectical mediation of its practice. It is
the bureaucracy itself which, in line with the extension of its
power, secretes class consciousness as its ideology. When he
writes *History and Class Consciousness*, Lukács is not anti-
Stalinist; he is within the same movement as Stalinism. He gives
the bureaucracy its philosophy of history, a reflexive philosophy
of class as subject by which the triumphant bureaucracy can
proceed historically to idealize its totalitarian practice.

of productive forces, labor, historical rationality, etc.? Evidently not. In this framework, the proletariat (or any other possible class) is pledged to enter into the rational dialectic of a form and a content (on the one hand, the structure of classes, on the other, its own class values, when these are not its class "interests"!). It is pledged to a *finality of class* that perfectly encloses it in the dialectical game of capitalist society.

Better still, by reinforcing itself in its being, in proportion to the development of the class struggle, it reinforces the power of the ruling class, and its degraded opposition serves the reformist impulse of the capitalist system, when it does not reveal itself as even more conservative in the realm of values. This is where we are today.

To what can we impute the historical blockage of the "revolutionary double negation" (the proletariat was well-born from the bourgeoisie, but it has not been born of itself as a class)? Lenin, even Stalin, the demise of the proletariat itself — are these dialectical accidents? Quite simply, the problem is the conjuncture of a revolutioanry theory aiming at the abolition of classes, outlined by Marx, with a revolutionary subject (the real and historical class of salaried workers). One cannot even say that the proletariat has slowly turned against itself. It has *logically* produced the substantialization of the social revolt in a theoretically untranscendable class, which was soon fixed in its being by the organization. Starting from there, the proletarian class and Marxist theory began *mutually to justify one another* and hence to *neutralize* each other. And the project of transforming life, as much the demand of Marx as that of the actual revolt, has placidly become the victory of the proletariat.

Revolution as Finality: History in Suspense

Along with the mode of production, the concept of history constitutes another index of this dialectical rationalization. It is a homologous concept developed in a social structure at the time of the theorization of the mode of production (once again, the imposition, during the Renaissance, of a perspectival convergence as the reality principle of space, serving as a reference).

One can speak of a millenarian element in Marx: 24 communism as a "proximate future," an imminent revolution. This "utopian" exigency dates from the *Introduction to the Critique of Hegel's Philosophy of Right*, the *1844 Manuscripts*, the *Theses on Feuerbach*, and the *Manifesto*. After the failures of 1848, there was a reconversion. Communism was no longer an immediate possibility of the present situation; it could become a real possibility only much later, *at the end of a period in which the necessary historical conditions will have been created.* 25 With *Capital*, one moves from the revolutionary utopia to a fully historical dialectic, from an immediate and radical revolt to an objective consideration of the situation. It is necessary that capitalism "mature," that it inwardly become a social system through its own negation. Hence there is a *logical and historical necessity*, a dialectical long march in which the negativity of the proletariat does not have an immediate effect on itself as a class but instead has a long-term effect on the process of capital. Engaged in this long "objective" detour, the

---

24.   We are referring to the work of Kalivoda, *Marx et Freud* (Paris: Editions anthropos,1971).

25.   The same holds in Christian history; the Christian concept of historicity is born from the failure of the parousia.

proletariat begins to reflect upon itself as the negation and as the subject of history.[26]

The effort of Marxism then diverges from its radical exigency toward the study of historical laws. The proletariat no longer leaps out of its shadow; it grows larger in the shadow of capital. The revolution is housed in an implacable process of evolution at the end of which the laws of history require man to liberate himself as a social creature. The Marxist perspective does not abandon its radical exigency but it becomes a *final* exigency. There is a conversion from the here-and-now to an asymptotic fulfillment, a *deferred due date*, indefinitely put off, which, under the sign of a historical reality principle (the objective socialization of society achieved by capital; the dialectical process of maturation of the "objective" conditions of the revolution), confirms the transcendence of an *ascetic* communism, a communism of sublimation and hope. In the name of an always renewed future—future of history, future of the dictatorship of the proletariat, future of capitalism and future of socialism—it demands more and more the sacrifice of the immediate and permanent revolution. Ascetic in relation to its own revolution, communism in effect profoundly suffers from not "taking its desires as reality."[27] (The transcendent dimension, the sublimation, is the same as

---

26. Socialism in a single country will be the realization of this qualification in which the proletariat is situated, of this substantialization of negativity in which history as the *final* dimension becomes the objective dimension. At first the negative subject of the historical dialectic, it is then simply the positive subject of a positivist history of the revolution. This great slippage is only possible and only explained by the passage from utopia to the historical "epoché."

27. One of the famous statements of the students during May, 1968. [Translator's note]

that of orthodox Christianity in opposition to the millenarian sects who wanted immediate fulfillment, here below. As we know, sublimation is repressive. It is the basis fo the power of the Church.)

The revolution becomes an *end,* not in any sense the radical exigency that presumes, instead of counting on a final totalization, that man is *already totally there* in his revolt. Such is the meaning of utopia, if one distinguishes it from the dreaming idealism to which the "scientific ones" take pleasure in reducing it, only the better to bury it. It rejects the schema, *diluting* the contradictions. This ideal structuration, that has room for a "Reason" of history, for a conscious and logical organization of *deferred* revolution—this dialectic very rapidly falls into the pure and simple schema of end and means. *The Revolution as "end" is in fact equivalent to the autonomization of the means.* What has happened is clear: it has the effect of stifling the current situation, of exorcizing immediate subversion, of diluting (in the chemical sense of the term) explosive reactions in a long term solution.

"Man should know to be satisfied with the perspective of his liberation. This is why 'revolutionary romanticism,' revolt 'hic et nunc' will continue to thrive until the Marxist perspective ceases to be only a perspective" (Kalivoda). But, starting from the moment when Marxism enters into the game of the objectivity of history, when it resigns itself to the *laws* of history and the dialectic, can it be anything more than a "perspective"? In the era when Marx began to write, workers were breaking machines. Marx did not write for them. He had nothing to say to them. In his eyes they were even wrong; it was the industrial bourgeoisie that was revolutionary. Theoretical lag does not at all explain it. This immanent revolt of the workers who broke machines has remained without explanation. With his dialectic, Marx was content to see them as mere babes in the woods. But the whole workers' movement until the Commune lived by this utopian exigency of immediate socialism (Dégacque, Courderoy, etc.). And they *were* such even in their defeat. For utopia is never written for the future; it is always already present. Marx himself, speaking of the future, speaks of it as a transcended phase. But from what Olympian point of view can one judge him correct *in advance*? The failure of these movements (in contrast to the "Marxist" revolutions of the 20th century) is not a valid argument. That would simply involve invoking the "reason" of history, an objective end that would not be able to account for the specificity of a social speech that is not finalized by a future dimension. It is there, in the verdict of history, that international communism today looks for the only proof of its truth, that is, even more than before, in a dialectical reason, but also in the immanence of the facts. At this level history is no longer even a process; it is simply a trial. And revolt is always condemned in a legal proceeding.

The Radicality of Utopia

In fact, Marx is right, "objectively" right, but this correctness and this objectivity were won, as in all science, only at the cost of a *miscomprehension*, a miscomprehension of the radical utopias contemporary with the *Manifesto* and *Capital*. In saying that Marx "objectively" theorized capitalist social relations, the class struggle, the movement of history, etc., one has claimed too much. In effect, Marx "objectified" the convulsion of a social order,

its current subversion, the speech of life and death,
the liberator of the very movement, in a long-term
dialectical revolution, in a spiraling finality that was
only the endless screw of political economy.[28]

The cursed poet, non-official art, and utopian
writings in general, by giving a current and
immediate content to man's liberation, should be
the very speech of communism, its direct prophecy.
They are only its bad conscience precisely because
in them something of man is *immediately* realized,
because they object without pity to the "political"
dimension of the revolution, which is merely the
dimension of its final postponement. They are the
equivalent, at the level of discourse, of the savage
social movements that were born in a symbolic
situation of rupture (symbolic—which means non-
universalized, non-dialectical, non-rationalized in
the mirror of an imaginary objective history). This is
why poetry (not Art) was fundamentally connected
only with the utopian socialist movements, with
"revolutionary romanticism," and never with
Marxism as such. It is because the content of
liberated man is, at bottom, of less importance than
the abolition of the separation of the present and the
future. The abolition of this form of time, the
dimension of sublimation, makes it impossible to
pardon the idealists of the dialectic, who are at the
same time the realists of politics. For them the

---

28. It is not true that Marx "dialectically transcended"
utopia by conserving its "project" in a "scientific" model of
revolution. Marx wrote of *the Revolution according to the law.*
He did not make a dialectical synthesis of its *necessary* date of
maturity and the impassioned, immediate utopian exigency of
the transfusion of social relations, because it is futile to claim a
dialectic between these two antagonistic positions. What
historical materialism did transcend while conserving was quite
simply political economy.

revolution must be distilled in history; it must come on time; it must ripen in the sun of the contradictions. That it could be there immediately is unthinkable and *insufferable*. Poetry and the utopian revolt have this radical presentness in common, this denegation of finalities; it is this actualization of desire no longer relegated to a future liberation, but demanded here, immediately, even in its death throes, in the extreme situation of life and death. Such is happiness; such is revolution. It has nothing to do with the political ledger book of the Revolution.

Contrary to Marxist analysis which posits man as dispossessed, as alienated and relates him to a total man, a total Other who is Reason and who is for the future (which is utopian, but in the bad sense of the term), which assigns to man a project of totalization, *utopia*, for its part, *would have nothing to do with the concept of alienation*. It regards every man and every society as already totally there, at each social moment, in its symbolic exigency. Marxism never analyzes the revolt, or even the movement of society except *as an intricate ornament of the revolution*, as a reality on the way toward maturation. This is a racism of perfection, of the finished stage of reason. It throws everything else into a nothingness of things transcended.[29] Marxism is still profoundly a philosophy, even its "scientific" stage, through all that remains in it of a vision of alienation. In terms of "alienation," the other side of "critical" thought is always a total essence that haunts a divided existence. But this metaphysics of the totality is not

---

29. One takes a long time to outline the sketch of a work which, once completed, would be returned to oblivion and nothingness. But this is all wrong for the sketch already contains the whole work, and this alone is the work.

at all opposed to the present reality of the division. It is complementary to it. For the subject, the prospect of recovering his transparence or his total "use value" at the end of history is just as religious a vision as the reintegration of essences. "Alienation" remains the imaginary of the subject, even of the subject of history. The subject will not become again a total man; he will not rediscover himself; today he has lost himself. The totalization of the subject is still the end of the end of the political economy of consciousness, confirmed by the identity of the subject, just as political economy is confirmed by the principle of equivalence. Instead of deluding men with a phantasm of their lost identity, of their future autonomy, this notion itself must be abolished.

What an absurdity it is to pretend that men are "other," to try to convince them that their deepest desire is to become "themselves" again! Each man is totally there at each instant. Society also is totally there at each instant. Courderoy, the Luddites, Rimbaud, the Communards, the people of the savage strikes, those of May, 1968 — in every case the revolution does not speak indirectly; they are the revolution, not concepts in transit. Their speech is symbolic and it does not aim at an essence. In these instances, there is speech before history, before politics, before truth, speech before the separation and the future totality. He is truly a revolutionary who speaks of the world as non-separated.

There is no possible or impossible. The utopia is here in all the energies that are raised against political economy. But this utopian violence does not accumulate; it is lost. It does not try to accumulate itself as does economic value in order to abolish death. It does not grasp for power. To enclose the "exploited" within the single historical possibility of taking power has been the worst diversion the revolution has ever taken. One sees here to what depths the axioms of political economy have undermined, pervaded and distorted the revolutionary perspective. Utopia wants speech against power and against the reality principle which is only the phantasm of the system and its indefinite reproduction. It wants only the spoken word; and it wants to lose itself in it.